Dear David,

We Wish you a ?.

a Half Birthday and Man

With Love & Best Wishes,
Pushpa & Sam.

OXFORD IN VERSE

The Editors

Glyn Pursglove was born and educated in Yorkshire, before graduating from St Peter's College, Oxford, in 1968. He currently teaches at the University of Wales in Swansea. His work on English poetry of the seventeenth century, and on contemporary poetry, has been widely published.

Alistair Ricketts graduated from Trinity College, Oxford, in 1972, and has worked in the Taylorian and Bodleian Libraries and on the Oxford dictionaries. He is now Librarian of St Peter's College, Oxford. His published work includes two collections of verse and translations.

OXFORD IN VERSE

Chosen and edited by
GLYN PURSGLOVE
and
ALISTAIR RICKETTS

Oxford, take thou these leaves of the Tree of Life; with eloquence
That thy immortal tongue inspires, present them to Albion:
Perhaps he may receive them, offer'd from thy loved hands.

William Blake, *Jerusalem*: 11

THE PERPETUA PRESS
OXFORD

First published in 1999
by the Perpetua Press
26 Norham Road, Oxford OX2 6SF

ISBN: 1 870882 14 8

Printed in Great Britain by Oxuniprint, Oxford University Press

CONTENTS

INTRODUCTION

It is perhaps only natural that Oxford should have inspired a substantial body of verse. Its history, its buildings and its rivers, its personalities and their rivalries offer ready subjects. Given Oxford's role in the education of thousands of young men (and latterly women), a good number of whom inevitably had literary inclinations, it is hardly surprising that so much should have been written about it. In earlier ages, when a competence in verse was a normal social accomplishment of the educated, it offered a ready medium in which to discuss the University and its affairs. This book is no more than a sampling of some very extensive material. (This is especially true where our own century is concerned.) While there is little between its covers which could be called great poetry, there is, we believe, correspondingly little which is not highly readable. Much that we have included offers fascinating glimpses of the social history of Oxford and Oxford's role in the larger cultural life of the nation.

In his verse monologue 'The Dying Patriot', James Elroy Flecker offers a vision of Oxford (along with 'the Kentish hills' and 'the golden sea of Wales') as one of the things the patriot must fight to defend:

Noon strikes on England, noon on Oxford town,
—Beauty she was statue cold—there's blood upon
   her gown:
Noon of my dreams, O noon!
Proud and godly kings had built her, long ago,
With her towers and tombs and statues all arow,
With her fair and floral air and the love that lingers
   there,
And the streets where the great men go.

Elsewhere, in 'Oxford Canal' (reprinted in this volume), Flecker offers a rather different perspective on the city:
When you have wearied of the valiant spires of this
   County Town,
Of its wide white streets and glistening museums,

and black monastic walls,
Of its red motors and lumbering trams, and self
    sufficient people,
I will take you walking with me to a place you have
    not seen—
Half town and half country—the land of the Canal.
It is dearer to me than the antique town.

In this collection we have sought to represent both
points of view. We include, naturally, many poems which
might carry as a kind of shared epigraph Matthew
Arnold's famous description of Oxford as 'that sweet City
with her dreaming spires' (*Thyrsis*). Sometimes such ide-
alizations are the product of youthful hope; less often
they arise as part of a sustained and knowledgeable rela-
tionship with the city; most frequently they are generated
by nostalgia. Not all poets looking back on their Oxford
youth have combined affection with realism in the way
that William Shenstone did in his 'Ode to Memory'
(1788). Shenstone invokes 'Memory! celestial maid' to

> . . . sketch with care the muse's bow'r,
>   Where *Isis* rolls her silver tide;
> Nor yet omit one reed or flow'r
>   That shines on *Cherwell*'s verdant side;
> If so thou may'st those hours prolong,
> When polish'd *Lycon* join'd my song.
>
> The song it 'vails not to recite—
>   But sure, to soothe our youthful dreams,
> Those banks and streams appear'd more bright
>   Than other banks, than other streams:
> Or by thy softening pencil shewn,
> Assume they beauties not their own?

Edward Benlowes identifies Oxford as 'the Muses Par-
adise'; Edwin Arnold, in a poem significantly entitled
'Oxford Revisited', celebrates it as the 'Fair and Queenly
One! / Tower-crowned, and girdled with . . . silver
streams'. Nicholas Amhurst, on the other hand, declares
that 'In Oxford Crouds of stupid Bards are found' and

Richard Polwhele, in the Oxford of the 1780s, finds a 'motley mercenary Herd' of clergymen, a 'shameless Tribe' of 'vile Hirelings'. The poets have not always taken a rosy view of Oxford, and we have tried to represent the critic as well as the celebrant.

To keep the book within reasonable proportions, we have had, inevitably, to be highly selective. There are many other poets and poems we would have liked to represent. Some of these are alluded to, where relevant, in the biographical notes which introduce each poet. Other omissions we regret range in time from 'The Miller's Tale' and 'The Clerk of Oxenford' in Chaucer's *Canterbury Tales* to W. N. Herbert's series of 'Poems from the Pitt Rivers' (*The Testament of the Reverend Thomas Dick*, 1994) and Roger Freebairn's 'Evening Out' (*Evening Out*, 1997). F. T. Prince's *Memoirs in Oxford* (1970) proved too long to include in full and too closely integrated to extract sensibly; a similar difficulty faced us with the Oxford poems in Hubert Moore's *Rolling Stock* (1991). We are sad, too, that we were finally unable to find room for poems by John Wain or David Constantine, such as his 'On Oxford Station, 15 February 1997' (*The Pelt of Wasps*, 1997). Nor are these the only contemporary poets to have tempted us: others include Gareth Reeves ('Oxford' in *Listening In*, 1993), Lotte Kramer ('Oxford, 1940s' in *The Desecration of Trees*, 1994) and Deirdre Shanahan ('Wedding at Christ Church Cathedral, Oxford' in *Legal Tender*, 1988). From the earlier part of the century our omissions have had to include Kipling's 'The Clerks and The Bells', Binyon's 'Oxford in War-Time', Auden's 'Oxford', Canto XIII of MacNeice's *Autumn Journal*, Drummond Allison's 'An Explanation of Oxford', and Dylan Thomas's entertaining lines on life in the grounds of Magdalen College (see James A. Davies, 'Dylan Thomas in Oxford: An Unpublished Poem' in *Notes and Queries*, September 1997). We might offer similar lists of poems from earlier centuries. Thus, though we have included a number of eighteenth- and nineteenth-century sonnets on Oxford, we have stopped short of filling 'whole volumes in folio' with them (to quote Shakespeare's Don Armado). There would certainly be material for such a volume—Arthur Hugh Clough's three 'Commemoration Sonnets, 1844', Thomas Herbert Warren's 'May-Day on Magdalen Tower', Keble's 'Oxford. From Bagley, at 8.a.m.', and numerous minor Victorians. From Bowles onwards, the 'Oxford sonnet' becomes a recognizable minor genre.

For all such omissions, we believe that the present pages offer a representative range of responses to Oxford over a period of some four hundred years. We begin with Thomas Lodge's vision of Christ Church Meadow peopled by dancing water nymphs and we end with Duncan Bush's annotation of 'the draughty common sink, the crumbling edge / Of Cotswold sills, the old decrepit stair'. Between the two we range from Samuel Austin and his 'most unintelligible poems' (as mocked by Thomas Flatman) to 'the stiff-necked proctors, wary-eyed, / The dons, the coaches, and the rest' (as observed by G. W. Thornbury), and from 'Cherwell's matted hawthorn bowers' (celebrated by F.W.Faber) to 'Council housing snug beside / Victorian pub and corner shop', judged by Jonathan Price to be a proper source of 'modest pride'. There are perhaps as many Oxfords as there are poets, and we have the word of one of those poets, Thomas Tickell, that

Parnassus owns its honours far outdone,
And Isis boasts more Bards than Helicon.

Glyn Pursglove
Alistair Ricketts

A Note on Texts

An 'Index of Sources Used' is provided at the end of the volume. Texts have been presented with the minimum of editorial interference. Some obvious errors have been corrected; in early texts the use of 'i' and 'j' and 'u' and 'v' has been regularized in accordance with modern practice.

THOMAS LODGE

(1558?–1625)

Lodge was born in West Ham and educated at Merchant Taylors' School before matriculating at Trinity College in 1573. He obtained his BA in 1577 and his MA four years later. He later studied medicine in France, and was awarded his MD in Oxford in 1602. His career as a writer spanned the years from 1580 to 1600. After his conversion to Catholicism he practised as a doctor. He made important contributions to Elizabethan fiction (e.g. *Rosalynde*, 1590), drama (e.g. *The Wounds of Civil War*, 1588?), and poetry. His narrative *Scillaes Metamorphosis* (of which the opening appears below) was printed in 1589 and is generally regarded as the first contribution to the distinctively Elizabethan genre of the Ovidian love narrative, later examples of which included Marlowe's *Hero and Leander* and Shakespeare's *Venus and Adonis*. The banks of the Isis provide the setting for the poem's opening, as Lodge draws on his years as a member of Trinity. Water nymphs perhaps dance in Christ Church Meadow less often now than they did in Lodge's days.

from *Scillaes Metamorphosis*

Walking alone (all onely full of griefe)
Within a thicket nere to Isis floud,
Weeping my wants, and wailing scant reliefe,
Wringing mine armes (as one with sorrowe wood);
    The piteous streames relenting at my mone
    Withdrew their tides, and staid to heare me grone.

From foorth the channell, with a sorrowing crie
The Sea-god Glaucus (with his hallowed heares
Wet in the teares of his sad mothers dye)
With piteous lookes before my face appeares;
    For whome the Nimphes a mossie coate did frame,
    Embroadered with his Sillas heavenly name.

And as I sat under a Willow tree,
The lovelie honour of faire Thetis bower;
Reposd his head upon my faintfull knee:
And when my teares had ceast their stormie shower
  He dried my cheekes, and then bespake him so,
  As when he waild I straight forgot my woe.

Infortunate, why wandreth thy content
From forth his scope as wearied of it selfe;
Thy bookes have schoold thee from this fond repent,
And thou canst talke by proofe of wavering pelfe:
  Unto the world such is inconstancie,
  As sapp to tree, as apple to the eye.

Marke how the morne in roseat colour shines,
And straight with cloudes the Sunnie tract is clad;
Then see how pomp through waxe and waine declines,
From high to lowe, from better to the bad:
  Take moist from Sea, take colour from his kinde,
  Before the world devoid of change thou finde.

With secret eye looke on the earth a while,
Regard the changes Nature forceth there;
Behold the heavens, whose course all sence beguile;
Respect thy selfe, and thou shalt find it cleere,
  That infantlike thou art become a youth,
  And youth forespent a wretched age ensu'th.

In searching then the schoolemens cunning noates,
Of heaven, of earth, of flowers, of springing trees,
Of hearbs, of mettall, and of Thetis floates,
Of lawes and nurture kept among the Bees:
  Conclude and knowe times change by course of fate,
  Then mourne no more, but moane my haples state.

Here gan he pause and shake his heavie head,
And fould his armes, and then unfould them straight;
Faine would he speake, but tongue was charm'd by
    dread,
Whil'st I that sawe what woes did him awaight,
    Comparing his mishaps and moane with mine,
    Gan smile for joy and drie his drooping eyne.

But (loe) a wonder; from the channels glide
A sweet melodious noyse of musicke rose,
That made the streame to dance a pleasant tide,
The weedes and sallowes neere the bancke that groes
    Gan sing, as when the calmest windes accorde
    To greete with balmie breath the fleeting forde.

Upon the silver bosome of the streame
First gan faire *Themis* shake her amber locks,
Whom all the Nimphs that waight on Neptunes realme
Attended from the hollowe of the rocks.
    In briefe, while these rare parragons assemble,
    The watrie world to touch their teates doo tremble.

Footing it featlie on the grassie ground,
These Damsels circling with their brightsome faires
The love-sicke God and I, about us wound
Like starres that *Ariadnes* crowne repaires:
    Who once hath seene or pride of morne, or day,
    Would deeme all pompe within their cheekes did
        play . . .

SIR JOHN HARINGTON

(1560–1612)

A godson of Queen Elizabeth, Harington was educated at Eton, King's College, Cambridge, and Lincoln's Inn. His career as a courtier was interrupted by two years of banishment after a suspected slur on the Earl of Leicester in 1596. Eventually his close association with the Earl of Essex put him out of favour with the Queen. He later became tutor to Prince Henry at the court of James I. His writings include his entertaining mock- encomium on the water-closet, *The Metamorphosis of Ajax* (1596), a magnificent translation of Ariosto's *Orlando Furioso* (1591), and many witty epigrams and shorter poems. He had a considerable and seemingly well-deserved reputation for wit and erudition. Many of his poems were published posthumously in *Nugae Antiquae* between 1769 and 1775; some of his political writings did not see the light until the nineteenth century.

Of Learning Nothing at a Lecture, upon Occasion of Dr
Reynolds at Oxford, afore my Lord of Essex, and divers
Ladies and Courtiers, at the Queenes last beeing there,
on these words: Idolunc nihil est, An Idol is nothing

While I at Oxford stay'd, some few months since,
To see, and serve our deare & Soveraigne Prince,
Where graciously her Grace did see and show
The choisest fruits that learning could bestow,
I went one day to heare a learned Lecture
Read (as some said) by *Bellarmines* correcter,
And sundry Courtiers more then present were,
That understood it well save here and there:
Among the rest, one whom it least concerned,
Askt me what I had at the Lecture learned?
I that his ignorance might soone be *guile*,
Did say, I learned nothing all the while.
Yet did the Reader teach with much facilitie,
And I was wont to learne with some docilitie.
What learn'd you, Sir, (quoth he) in swearing moode?
I nothing learn'd, for nought I understood,
I thanke my Parents, they, when I was yong,
Barr'd me to learne this Popish Romane tong,

4

And yet it seemes to me, if you say true,
I without learning learn'd the same that you;
Most true, said I, yet few dare call us Fooles,
That this day learned nothing at the Schooles.

MICHAEL DRAYTON

(1563–1631)

Born in Warwickshire, Drayton appears to have been a page to
Henry Goodere by 1573. By the early 1590s he was living in
London, writing and publishing poetry and plays. He worked
in many genres, including love poetry, pastorals, historical nar-
ratives, religious poetry, and Ovidian narrative, and in many
verse forms, such as sonnets, heroic couplets, and ottava rima.
He had connections with the Children of the King's Revels at
Whitefriars from 1607 to 1612. In that last year he was in Prince
Henry's household. His *Polyolbion* (1612–22) is a massive ex-
pression of his love for his native country in which he seeks to
provide, poetically, a '*chorographical* description of *Tracts, Rivers,
Mountaines, Forests*, and other Parts of . . . Great Britaine, With
intermixture of the most Remarquable *Stories, Antiquities, Won-
ders, Rarityes, Pleasures, and Commodoties* of the same'. An alto-
gether lighter touch is evident in his fairy poem 'Nymphidia'.
He was buried in Westminster Abbey.

from *Polyolbion*

>   . . . *Isis* from her sourse
> Comes tripping with delight, downe from her daintier
>   Springs:
> And in her princely traine, t'attend her Marriage, brings
> Cleere *Churnet, Colne*, and *Leech*, which first she did
>   retaine,
> With *Windrush*: and with her (all out-rage to restraine
> Which well might offred be to *Isis* as shee went)
> Came *Yenload* with a guard of Satyres, which were sent
> From *Whichwood*, to await the bright and God-like
>   Dame.
> So, *Bernwood* did bequeath his Satyres to the *Tame*,
> For Sticklers in those stirres that at the feast should bee.
>   These preparations great when *Cherwell* comes to see,
> To *Oxford* got before, to entertaine the Flood,
> *Apollo's* ayde he begs, with all his sacred brood,
> To that most learned place to welcome her repaire.
> Who in her comming on, was wext so wondrous faire,
> That meeting, strife arose betwixt them, whether they
> Her beauty should extoll, or shee admire their Bay.

On whom their severall gifts (to amplifie her dowre)
The Muses there bestowe; which ever have the power
Immortal her to make. And as shee past along,
Those modest *Thespian* Maids thus to their *Isis* song;
   Yee Daughters of the Hills, come downe from every side,
And due attendance give upon the lovely Bride:
Goe strew the paths with flowers by which shee is to
   passe.
For be yee thus assur'd, in *Albion* never was
A beautie (yet) like hers: where have yee ever seene
So absolute a Nymph in all things, for a Queene?
Give instantly in charge the day be wondrous faire,
That no disorderd blast attempt her braided haire.
Goe, see her State prepar'd, and every thing be fit,
The bride-chamber adorn'd with all beseeming it.
And for the princely groome, who ever yet could name
A Flood that is so fit for *Isis* as the *Tame*?
Yee both so lovely are, that knowledge scarce can tell,
For feature whether hee, or beautie shee excell:
That ravished with joy each other to behold,
When as your crystall wasts you closely doe enfold,
Betwixt your beautious selves you shall beget a Sonne,
That when your lives shall end, in him shall be begunne.
The pleasant *Surryan* shores shall in that Flood delight,
And *Kent* esteeme her selfe most happy in his sight.
The Shire that *London* loves, shall onely him prefer,
And give full many a gift to hold him neer to her.
The *Skeld*, the goodly *Mose*, the rich and Viny *Rheine*,
Shall come to meet the *Thames* in *Neptunes* watry Plaine.
And all the *Belgian* Streames and neighboring Floods of
   Gaul,
Of him shall stand in awe, his tributaries all.
   As of fayre *Isis* thus, the learned Virgins spake,
A shrill and suddaine brute this *Prothalamion* brake;
That *White-horse*, for the love she bare to her Ally,
And honored sister Vale, the bountious *Alsbury*,
Sent Presents to the *Tame* by *Ock* her onely Flood,
Which for his Mother Vale, so much on her greatnesse
   stood.
   From *Oxford*, *Isis* hasts more speedily . . .

SAMUEL DANIEL

(c.1562–1619)

Daniel was born near Taunton, the son of a music-master. He entered Magdalen Hall, Oxford in 1581, but left without taking a degree. His marriage made him a brother-in-law of John Florio. He accompanied Lord Stafford, the English Ambassador to France in 1586; during 1590–1 he was in Italy with Sir Edward Dymoke. He spent some time as tutor to William Herbert, Lady Anne Clifford, and other members of the Pembroke and Herbert families; he held a series of posts at the court of James I, in the service of Queen Anne. As a lyric poet and sonneteer, and as a composer of historical narratives and court masques, he was never less than highly competent, often much more than merely competent, *pace* Ben Jonson's judgement that he was 'a good honest man . . . but no poet'. In prose, his *Defence of Rhyme* (1603) and his *Collection of the History of England* (1618) display his learning, his intelligence, and his capacity for lucid expository prose.

S. D. To his Booke, in the dedicating thereof to the Librarie in Oxford, erected by Sir Thomas Bodley Knight

Heere in this goodly Magazine of witte,
This Storehouse of the choisest furniture
The world doth yeelde, heer in this exquisite,
And most rare monument, that dooth immure
The glorious reliques of the best of men;
Thou part imperfect worke, voutsafed art
A little roome, by him whose care hath beene
To gather all what ever might impart
Delight or Profite to Posteritie;
Whose hospitable bountie heere receives
Under this roofe powers of Divinitie,
Inlodg'd in these transformed shape of leaves.
For which good Worke his Memorie heere lives,
As th'holy guardian of this reverent place,
Sacred to Woorth, being fit that hee which gives
Honour to others, should himselfe have grace.
    And charitable BODLEY that hath thus
Done for the good of these, and other times,

Must live with them, and have his fame with us.
For well wee see our groveling fortune climes
Up to that sphere of glory, to be seene
From farre, by no course else, but by this way
Of dooing publique good; this is the meane
To shew we were, how fram'd, of what good clay.
For well we see how private heapes (which care
And greedy toyle provides for her owne endes)
Doe speede with her succeeders, and what share
Is left of all that store, for which it spendes
It selfe, not having what it hath in use,
And no good t'others nor it selfe conferres:
As if that Fortune mocking our abuse
Would teach us that it is not ours, but hers
That which we leave: and if we make it not
The good of many, she will take that paine,
And re-dispers th'inclosed parcelles got
From many hands, t'in-common them againe.
Which might advise us, that our selves should doe
That worke with judgement, which her blindnesse will,
And passe a State which she cannot undoe,
And have th'assurance in our owne name still.
    For this is to communicate with men
That good the world gave by societie,
And not like beasts of prey, draw all to' our Den
T'inglut our selves, and our owne progenie.
This is to make our giftes immortall giftes,
And thankes to last, whilst men, and bookes shall last;
This heritage of glory never shiftes
Nor changes Maisters; what thou leav'st thou hast.
The grounds, the lands, which now thou callest thine,
Have had a thousand lords that term'd them theirs,
And will be soone againe pent from thy line,
By some concussion, change, or wastefull heires.
We can no perpetuitie collate
Upon our race that ever will endure;
It is the worlds demaines, whereof no state
Can be by any cunning made so sure,
But at the change of Lordes for all our paine,
It will returne unto the world againe.

9

And therefore did discreet Antiquitie,
Heere (seeing how ill mens private cares did speede),
Erect an everlasting Granery
Of Artes, the universall State to feede,
And made the worlde their heire, whereby their name
Holdes still a firme possession in the same.
O well given landes, wherein all the whole land
Hath an eternall share! where every childe
Borne unto Letters, may be bolde to stand
And claime his portion, and not be beguilde.
Happy erected walles whose reverent piles
Harbour all commers, feede the multitude:
Not like the prowd-built pallace that beguiles
The hungry soule with empty solitude;
Or onely raisde for private luxurie
Stands as an open marke for Envies view,
And being the purchase of felicitie
Is Fortunes in remainder, as her due.
But you, blest you, the happy monuments
Of Charitie and Zeale, stand and beholde
Those vaine expences, and are documents
To shew what glory hath the surest holde.
You tell these times, wherein kind Pietie
Is dead intestate, and true noble Worth
Hath left no heire, that all things with us die,
Save what is for the common good brought forth.
    Which this judicious Knight did truely note,
And therefore heere hath happily begunne
To shew this age, that had almost forgot
This way of glory, and thereby hath wonne
So much of Time, as that his memorie
Will get beyond it, and will never die.

JOHN DAVIES OF HEREFORD
(1565?–1618)

Though probably never actually a member of the University, Davies certainly worked in Oxford as a writing-master, and seems to have drawn many of his pupils from Magdalen College. He published extensively and variously. *Wittes Pilgrimage* of 1605 promises the reader 'Amorous sonnets, soule-passions, and other Passages, divine, philosophicall, morall, poeticall, and politicall', and the mixture is characteristic. Some of his best work is to be found among his satires, as in *The Scourge of Folly* (1611). His handbook, *The Writing Schoolemaster* (c.1625), contains some handsome engraved plates.

To My Most Deere and Best Beloved Patronesse, Magdalen Colledge in Oxford

O honyed *Magdalen*! sweete, past compare
Of all the blisfull Heav'ns, on *Earth* that are:
Happy are they that in thee live at rest,
As free from *Ignorance*, as *State-distrest*.
O that I had an *Angells* tongue to mount
Thy praise beyond the pitch of high'st account.
Store makes me scarce; I have, and have not words
To royallize thy fame, as *Fame* affords:
For *Fame* and *Fortune* both together strives
To crowne thy *Praise* with rich *superlatives*.
(Meere *Abysse* of terene felicity!
Divine Inchantresse of the *Eare* and *Eye*)
The Wings wherewith thou mount'st thy self above
Are Wealth and Arte, and what else causeth love.
Live long togeather Head, and Corps, and all
That's yours directly, or Collaterall:
I have no *Guifts* your *Grace* to amplifie;
But must, with myne advice, the same supply:
Take heed how you disjoyne, or fall at strife;
For, I observe all *fortunes* in this life;
And of them all which I have seene or prov'd,
Yours onely yours, deserves to be belov'd.

WILLIAM GAMAGE

(1584– ?)

The William Gamage whose name appears on the title-page of *Linsie-Woolsie, Or, Two Centuries of epigrammes* was probably the same William Gamage who matriculated in 1604 at Jesus College, Oxford, 'aged 20'. The Oxford records describe him as being from Glamorgan, and in 1614 he became vicar of Eglwysiliam in the same county. Many of the more than two hundred epigrams in *Linsie-Woolsie* contain references to Welsh people or places. There are indications, too, of his social connections and aspirations—of his distant links with the Sidneys and Herberts—and of his friends, in poems such as 'To his friend Mr. Hop: for the loane of Dod, and Cleaner on the Decalogue' and 'To his lo: fr. Mr. W. Aubrey, an ingenious Anagramatist, late turned a Minister'.

In the Praise of Brasen-Nose-Coll.

Thy Nose more famous is, tho't be of Brasse,
Then many a head of many a golden Asse.

Tom of Christ Church in Oxford. To our Ceremonious Papists.

The clapping sound of Antichristian Bels,
They say, expels from them their airie Ghosts:
So, *Tom*, thy sound which all thy mates excels,
Doth thine Oxonians cause to flie their Hoasts.
But if thy sound could sound as far as Spaine,
Their bodies Ghosts, I thinke, would them refraine.

RICHARD CORBETT

(1582–1635)

Corbett's father Vincent, famed for his skill as a gardener, is celebrated in Ben Jonson's 'An Epitaph on Master Vincent Corbet'. The younger Corbett was educated at Westminster School before entering, in 1598, Broadgates Hall (later to be Pembroke College) and, a year later, Christ Church. Corbett soon became a well-known wit of the University; Wood speaks of his reputation for 'poems, jests, romantic fancies and exploits'. Some, at least, of his 'exploits' had connections with his fondness for alcohol. This did not prevent his advancement. In 1612 he was made Junior Proctor of the University and delivered a well-received Latin oration on the death of Prince Henry. In 1620 he became Dean of Christ Church, in 1628 Bishop of Oxford, and in 1635 Bishop of Norwich. His character seems not to have changed substantially, for all his ecclesiastical advancement. One of his two chaplains was William Strode; the other was Thomas Lushington, said to be 'more ingenious than prudent'. Aubrey tells us that Corbett and Lushington 'loved one another. The bishop sometimes would take the key of the wine-cellar and he and his chaplain would go and lock themselves in and be merry. Then first he lays down his episcopal hat — "there lies the Doctor." Then he putts of his gowne, — "There lyes the Bishop." Then 'twas, "Here's to thee, Lushington."' ('Great Tom' is a bell in Tom Tower in Christ Church. It weighs 7.5 tonnes and is tolled 101 times every night; it formerly served as a curfew bell, the number 101 representing the original number of scholars at Christ Church. Corbett's poem asserts its superiority over other bells, in Oxford and elsewhere.)

On John Dawson, Butler at Christ Church

Dawson the butler's dead; although I thinke
Poets were nere infusd with single drinke
Ile spend a farthing muse, some wat'ry verse
Will serve the turne to cast uppon this herse,
If any cannot weepe amongst you here
Take off his pott & soo squeeze out a teare
Weepe o his cheeses, weepe till you be good,
Ye that are dry, or in the sun have stood
In mossy coats & rusty liveries mourne
Untill like him to Ashes ye shall turne

Weepe o ye barrells lett your drippings fall
In trinkling streames, make wast more prodigall
Then when our drinke is bad, that John may floate
To Stix in beare, & lift up Charons boate
With wholesome waves, & as our cunduits run
With clarret at the coronation,
Soe lett oure channells flow with single tiffe
For John I trust is crownd; take off your whiffe
Ye men of rosemary, now drinke off all
Remembringe tis the butlers funerall
    Had he bin master of good double beere
    My Life for his, John Dawson had bin heere.

On Great Tom of Christ-Church

Be dumbe, ye infant chimes. Thumpe not your mettle
Which nere out range a tinker and his kettle;
Cease all your pettie larumes, for to-day
Is younge Toms resurection from the clay,
And knowe when Tom shall ringe his loudest knells
The bigst of you'le bee thought but dinner bells.

Old Tom's growne younge againe; the firy cave
Is now his cradle that was erst his grave.
He grewe up quickly from his mother earth
And all you see it is not an houres birth.
Looke on him well: my life I dare engage
You nere saw prettier babie of his age.

Sum take his measure by the rule; sum by
The Jacobs staffe take his profunditie,
And sume his altitude: some boldly sweare
Yonge Tom's not like the old, but Tom, nere feare
The Critick Geometritians line
If thou as loude as ere thou didst ringe nine.

14

Miles, what's the matter? alle thus out of square?
I hope St Marys hall won't longe forbeare
Your coxcomes pate; their clocke hangs dume ins tower
And knowes not that 4 quarters make an houre.
Now Brontes joyes ringe out; the churlish cur
Nere laughs abroade till greate belles catch the mur.

Tom did noe soner peepe from under grounde
But strait St Marys Tennor lost his sound.
O how his maypole founders hart did swell
With full moone tides of joy when the cracked bell
Choaked with envie and his admiration,
Runge like a quarte pot to the congregation.

This punie bell is proude and hopes noe other,
But that in time he shall be grate Tom's brother.
Thou art wise in this thou wishest; bee it soe,
Let one Hen hatch you both; for thus much knowe:
He that did cast Ch: Ch: greate Tom soe well
Can easier cast St Maryies bigest bell.

Rejoyce with Ch: Ch:. Looke higher Osny,
Of giant bells the famoust tresury.
The base vast thundringe clocke of Whestminster,
Grand Tom of Lincolne, and huge Exeter,
Are but Toms oldest brothers, and perchance
He may call coson with the bell in France.

Nere greive, old Oseny, at thy heavie fall.
Thy reliques bild thee up againe, they all
Florish thy great glorie; theire sole fame
When thou art not, will keepe great Osneys name.
This Tom was infant of thy mightie steeple,
Yet hee is Lord Controuler of a people.

Tom lately went his progresse and looks ore
What he nere saw in manie yeares before,
And when he sawe the old foundation
And litell hope had he of preparation,
He burst with greef and least he should not have
Due pompe, hee's his owne Bell man to the grave.

And that there might of Tom be still stronge mention
He caried to his grave a new invention:
They drew his brounde bread face on pretie gins,
And made him stalke upon two rowlinge pins;
But Sander Hill sware twice or thrice by heaven,
He nere got such a lofe into the oven.

And Tom did Sanders vex, his ciclops maker,
As much as hee did Sander Hill the baker;
Thearfore loude thumpinge Tom be this thy pride,
That thou this motto should have on thy side:
Great world one Alexander conquered thee,
And two as mightie men scarce conquered mee.

Brave constant spirit, none could make thee turne,
Though hanged, drawne, quartred, till they made thee
    burne;
Nor yet for this nor ten times bee thou sory,
Since thou art martyred for the churches glory.
But for thy meritorious sufferings
Thou shortely shalst reward heaven in a stringe,
And though we grieved to see thee thumpt and bangd,
Yet weele be glad, greate Tom, to see thee hangd.

RICHARD BRATHWAITE

(1588?–1673)

Brathwaite was the son of a barrister who was Recorder of Kendal. He became a commoner of Oriel College in 1604. He remained at Oxford for some years, followed by a spell in Cambridge. Moving to London he took up the literary life, but on the death of his father in 1610 he returned to Westmoreland. He later became a Justice of the Peace and a Deputy Lieutenant of the county. 1611 saw his first publication (*The Golden Fleece, whereto bee annexed two elogies, Narcissus change and Aesons dotage*) and for more than fifty years he continued to publish extensively. Epigrams and pastorals, satires and odes came equally readily to him; he published works on drinking and smoking, translations, courtesy books, works of religion, and much else. He was and is best-known for *Barnabœ Itinerarium or Barnabee's Journal* (1636–38), an entertaining verse narrative in Latin and English of a journey around England, in which inns and public houses feature prominently. (A copesmato is a colleague or an associate.)

from *Barnabee's Journal*

To *Banbery* came I, O prophane one!
Where I saw a Puritane-one,
Hanging of his Cat on Monday,
For killing of a Mouse on Sonday.

To Oxford came I, whose Copesmato
Is *Minerva*, Well of *Plato*;
From which Seat doe streame most seemlie
Aganippe, *Hippocrene*;
Each thing ther's the *Muses Minion*,
Queenes College-Horn speakes pure *Athenian*.

Thence to *Godsto*, with my Lovers,
Where a Tombe a Strumpet covers;
ROSAMUND lies there interred,
Flesh to dust and shade's compared,
Lye he 'bove, or lye she under,
To be buried is no wonder.

Thence to *Woodstock* I resorted,
There a Labyrinth's reported,
But of that no 'count I tender,
I found an Hostesse quicke and slender:
And her Guests more sweetly eying,
Than a thousand *Rosamunds* dying . . .

*To the Famous Seminary of all accomplish'd knowledge,
his deare Foster-Mother, the Universitie of Oxford; the
happie supplie of judicious witts, with the encrease of all
succeeding honour*

To thee (deare Mother) in whose learned lap,
I once repos'd, and from whose batt'ning papp
I suckt the milke of knowledge, send I *these*

Which if they please, as I could wish them please
I'me honor'd by *them*, and will still renew
My love to *them*, because they'r lik'd by *you*.
But *these* are feeble, scarce Penfeathered,
And like young *Lapwings* run with shell on head;
Nor can I blame them: for belike they've heard,
How I was young when I to *you* repair'd:
Growing in some sort riper; and *these* doe
Expect the like, that they shall thrive so too:
Which I confesse lies onely in your power,
For if you smile *they live*, *die* if you *loure*;
Nor need I feare, for I did never know
Any darke *Cloud* sit on your *smoother* brow.

Yours in all endeared observance, R. B.

18

JAMES HOWELL
(1594?–1666)

Howell was born at Llangammarch in Breconshire, where his father was curate. He was educated at Hereford Free School and, from 1610, at Jesus College, Oxford, of which he was made a Fellow in 1623. After 1616 he spent some years on the Continent. His skill in languages led to his involvement in a number of diplomatic missions; in 1622–24 he was visiting Spain and Sardinia, in 1632 he was at the Danish court. He was MP for Richmond, in Yorkshire, in 1628–29. After 1639 he acted as a secret agent for Strafford, leading to his imprisonment in the Fleet from 1643 to 1651. At the Restoration his services to the Royal party were recognized in his appointment as the first King's Historiographer. An excellent Latinist, Howell also compiled *Lexicon Tetraglotton: An English-French-Italian-Spanish Dictionary* (1660). His many other publications included political pamphlets, historical and philological works, poems, and a number of translations. He is now best-known for his *Epistolae Ho-Elianae: Familiar Letters Domestic and Forren* (1645–55), entertaining discussions of men and manners, places and ideas, studded with lively anecdotes.

To my Dear Mother the University of Oxford, upon Mr Cartwright's Poems

Alma Mater,

Many do suck thy Breasts, but *now* in *som*
Thy milk turns into *froth* and spumy *scum*;
In *Others* it converts to *rheum* and *steam*,
Or some poor *wheyish* stuff in stead of cream;
In Som it doth *malignant* humors breed,
And make the head turn round as that-side *Tweed*;
These humors vapor up unto the brains,
And so break forth to odd fanatic strains;
It makes them dote and rave, fret, fume and foam,
And strangely from their Texts in Pulpits roam,
When they should speak of *Rheims*, they prate of
    Rome,
Their theam is *birch*, their preachment is of *broom*:
Nor 'mong the *Forders* only such are found,
But they who pass the Bridg are quite as Round.

Som of thy *Sons* prove Bastards, sordid, base,
Who having suck'd *Thee* throw dirt in thy face,
When they have squeez'd thy Nipples, and chast
    Papps,
They dash thee on the Nose with frumps and rapps;
They grumble at thy Commons, Buildings, Rents,
And would bring Thee to farthing *Decrements;*
Few by thy *milk sound nutriment* now gain
For want of good *concoction* of the brain.

But this choice Son of thine is no such *brat,*
Thy *Milk* in him did so coagulat
That it became *Elixar,* as we see
In these mellifluous *streams* of Poesie.

WILLIAM STRODE

(c.1602–1645)

Born near Plympton in Devon, Strode attended Westminster
School before entering Christ Church in 1617. In 1618 he acted
in Robert Burton's *Philophaster* at Christ Church. Once ordained
in 1628, he became chaplain to Richard Corbett, Bishop of Ox-
ford, an older product of Westminster and Christ Church. In
1629 Strode was appointed Proctor and Public Orator of the
University. 'I saw faire Chloris' was a poem immensely popular
with Strode's contemporaries, to judge by the frequency with
which it appears in anthologies and miscellanies, both printed
and manuscript. In some manuscripts (e.g. MS. Rawl. poet. 160,
MS. Lat. Misc. c. 19, both in the Bodleian) the poem carries titles
such as 'On Dr: Corbets wife' or 'Dr Stroud on Mrs Corbett
Walking in the Snow'. Corbett, some nineteen years older than
Stroud, had married Alice Hutton, daughter of Leonard Hut-
ton, Canon of Christ Church. Alice Corbett, *née* Hutton, was fa-
mously beautiful. Aubrey characteristically mixes praise of her
beauty with scandal: 'He [Richard Corbett] married Alice Hut-
ton, whom 'twas sayd he bigott. She was a very beautiful
woman, and so was her mother.' Alice Corbett died of smallpox
in April 1628 (Strode composed three Latin elegies). 'I saw faire
Chloris' was evidently Strode's admiring, but tactful, praise of
his friend and colleague's wife, glimpsed (in imagination or in
reality) walking through an Oxford snowfall.

> I saw fair Chloris walk alone,
> Whilst feathered rain came softly down,
> And Jove descended from his tower
> To court her in a silver shower.
> The wanton snow flew on her breast
> Like little birds unto their nest;
> But overcome with whiteness there,
> For grief it thawed into a tear;
> Thence falling on her garment's hem,
> To deck her froze into a gem.

EDWARD BENLOWES

(1602–1676)

Benlowes was born into a Catholic family of some substance and, at the age of eleven, inherited an estate and a sizeable income. He was educated at St John's College, Cambridge, and became an Anglican.The years from 1627 to 1630 he spent travelling on the Continent. Back at home he was a friend and patron of many poets. Fines and levies imposed upon him as a supporter of the King began to sap his fortunes. A series of mishaps in the 1650s—a fire, being swindled over the sale of property—compounded his financial difficulties. He left his estate in Essex to live in London and then at Mapledurham. Eventually, at the end of 1666 or the beginning of 1667, he was arrested for debt and imprisoned in Oxford Castle. When released he took lodgings in Oxford and spent the rest of his life there, in some poverty, spending his time, according to Anthony à Wood, 'in the public library [i.e. the Bodleian], and conversation with ingenious scholars'. Many wondered at his unworldliness. In such circumstances he celebrated Oxford in his *Oxonii Encomium* of 1672, made up of three Latin poems and this in English. He was buried in St Mary's church.

On Oxford,
The Muses Paradise

1

Leave, bashfull Muse, the too hot Latian Shore,
   To Albions temperate Clime sail or'e;
     Sing *Learnings* Tempe, where clear *Oxfords* Eye,
       Like a bright rising Morn,
         Do's round herself descry
         What may a pleasant Seat adorn;
         Whither old Athens moves
      With all its Shades, and Walks, and Groves,
      With all its Pleasures, All its Arts,
Blessings, which to her *Darling* she imparts:
   Where sweet-breath'd Zephyr spreads his balmy wing
     Over her Eastern Garden, rich and fair,
       Where Winter represents a Spring;
         Which, stor'd with All that's rare,
         So riots with Encrease,
   As if Foecundity it self had sign'd the Lease;
        Whence issues such a fragrant Smell
        As might a Phoenix-Coffin parallel,
        And, were She here to dye again, might serve as
         well:
   Cool Breezes there fro neighbouring streams
     asswage
   That sultry Month in which mad Sirius breaths its
     Rage:
   Phoebus more gladly bends his western Head
To view those Walks, and Streams, than Thetis watry
   Bed.

Let Folly boast Elysian Plains,
    Chimera's of Romantick brains;
        Where Opall Gems on Cedars grow,
           Where Shrubs weep Gums, and Balm,
           The Aire perfum'd, and calm,
Where fresh Delights, smooth as its Rivers, flow
    With golden Sands, and pearly streams,
        With Amber-foam, and Diamond-gravel:—Dreams,
        Wild Rosy-crucian Themes,
Which cheat this World with fond Conceits of One
        below:
    Delicious Oxford, we presume,
    Makes good their feign'd Elysium;
        Where Plenty Avarice does cloy,
          And Appetite destroy:
        Natures full Breasts distill such Cheer,
          That Cattle need not envy here
The shining Ram and Bull plac'd in the starry Sphear:
    May still Exuberance so blesse
        This fertile Vale, that we may guess
          Rather from hence to Greece
Than from old Colchos, came the famous Golden Fleece.

Have you beheld Euganean Fields,
　Where Petrarch spent, and yet enlarg'd his Dayes?
　That Tempe Baths, Groves, Mountlets yields,
　　Natures green Silk each Hedge arrays;
　　Proud Medowes there
　　Embroidred Mantles wear;
　　Kind Summer, what each Spring engag'd for,
　　　payes:
There Plenty crowns the rolling Years,
　Shed from the Influence of the Spheres;
There Birds in Fleets sail through the Air (their Sea)
　Warbling sweet Notes on every Key,
Answer'd by Oat-pipes of each harmless Swain,
　　Under their Beechy Canopy;
　　A sweet, and innocent Security!
　　Health being their Feast, Content their Gain,
They view their Lambs dance on the verdant Plain;
　Old russet Honesty dwells there,
　All hearty, All sincere;
And yet, in this their Self-enjoying Reign,
　Although they Care, and Age beguil'd,
Slow-envious-wrinckles durst appear,
　Because so oft they smil'd:
While there I did Earths flowrie Carpet view,
　(Where Violets round the Primrose grew)
Me-thought a new-ris'n Sun in's azure Sphere did shew.

4

As There, so Here is All that may invite
 A longing Eye, or craving Appetite:
   Farmers, and Fields, round *Thee*, express
   In mutuall Smiles Their Happiness;
Two Thousand Sorts of Plants thy Physick-Garden dress,
 Where *Nature* in Her Self takes full Delight.
  As, when Apollo did on Daphne look,
    He at first View was strook;
   Shee, strangely arm'd with Beauty, did subdue
    (Strange Pow'r of Beauties Charms,
    'Bove Rhetorick, or Arms!)
The mighty *Conqu'rour* Who the Python slew:
 So, Who Thy *Theater*, Great *Sheldon*, view,
   And *Bodley*'s stately learned *Pile*,
  Where also *Seldens* Heap of Wonders lye,
   Arts triple *Pantheon*, Wisdoms *Pansophy*,
They stand amaz'd at This ore-comming *Sight*.
  Endeed, were Private Libraries not here,
   Those might the Name of Publike bear,
    Which we may well each Colledg-Treasure call,
    Did not their Living Libraries out-vie Them all;
    All, but their Glorious *Chappels*, Those we style
    Most Sacred *Arks*.—All, joyn'd together, may
Approachers, ev'n as Sheba's Queen, surprize
   With high Delight, and Them with greatest Wonder stay;
    Who would, thus ravish'd, ne're retire
   From gazing still on what they still admire,
Esteeming these fair Starres 'bove thousand Daphnean
 eyes;
   This Galaxie, that cleers the way
   To th' *Empire* of *Eternal Day*,
   Much more enlightens, quickens Us, and
   warms,
Than Sol that gilds the World, and carries Time in's
 Arms.

5

The Choicest Face by *Nature* pensil'd, seems
  Short-liv'd, as flow'rs, and rudely looks,
    Till rais'd by wise Convers, and wiser *Books*;
      Thou, *Knowledge*, giv'st to Beauty lasting
        Beams:
      When by *Arts* Chymistrie bright *Spirits* mount,
      The Skin-deep Whites, and Reds subside
        below;
Beauties still-ripening Fruit, in Wise Account,
  Do's on The *Tree* of *Knowledge* grow;
      Which, to Embrightned *Minds* more Glorie
        brings,
      Than Gems that blaze on Fronts of *Kings*.
      Fools from Times Lott'ry draw dull blanks of
        sport;
        Mules are but Mules, though trapp'd with
          Gold,
      And gallant Ignorants but poor, who want
Themselves,
        Ship-wrack'd on Follies Shelves:
        Bewitch'd with tinsel shew, and senseless
          noise,
With worthless, ill-presaging toyes.
    But They to whom Indulgent Heav'n
    This twofold Excellence has giv'n,
To Know, and wisely Act, They keep their Princely Court
    Within; Whose glorious Reign may be admir'd, not
        told;
        For Lifes long Age They wise Improvements
          choose,
When Folly has short hours, and has them but to loose.

Rude World! knew'st thou what Spring-Tide flowes
　　Of Mentall Joyes to Sons of Art, and Fame,
　　　　Who, active still, as Light, tread Aire and
　　　　Flame,
　　　　(Where Thirty Thousand Books in Order'd
　　　　Rows,
　　　　The Generall Councel of Fames Priests, do stand,
　　　　The living Shrines of *Worthies* dead)
Thou would'st then pine with Envie, or with Rage be
　　burst,
　　　　　Ev'n by Thy-self Accurst.
　　　　But here, Benign Stars, from your Blessed
　　　　Station
　　　　Ye brightly dart your Beams, Illustrious *Souls*!
　　　　In your refulgent Constellation
Are Thousand Lights into One Brightness spread;
　　From Your, the Best, and Noblest Conversation
　　　　Sweet Influ'ence round our Happy Island rolls;
　　　　By You, as streams by Nursing Springs, We'are
　　　　fed.
Then Justly may You, Bay-crown'd *Lords*, command
　　This due, and easie Tribute from our gratefull Hand.
　　　　We have faire Padua, Lovain, Leyden seen;
　　　　At Theirs, as *Oxford*, at Your *Lectures*, been;
They *Arts* Chief Maids of Honour are,—But You
　　　　Arts Qveen.

JOHN MILTON
(1608–1674)

translated
by

WILLIAM COWPER
(1731–1800)

Milton's Latin poem 'Ad Joannem Rousium Oxoniensis Acade-
miae Bibliothecarium' was composed in January 1647. In the
Bodleian Library (MS. Lat. Misc. f. 15) is a fair copy of this
poem, pasted into a copy of Milton's Poems of 1645. Rouse,
who became Bodley's Librarian in 1620, famously refused in
1645 to allow Charles I to borrow a book from the library. Mil-
ton was himself a graduate of Christ's College, Cambridge. In
this Latin poem his use of classical metres is highly unorthodox,
which is what lies behind Cowper's remarks in the headnote
written for his translation. Cowper was educated at Westmin-
ster School, after which he took chambers in the Middle Tem-
ple, before the first signs of the mental instability which was to
mark the rest of his life.

An Ode addressed to Mr. John Rouse, Librarian of the
University of Oxford. On a Lost Volume of my Poems,
which he desired me to replace, that he might add them
to my other Works deposited in the Library

[Note: This Ode is rendered without rhime, that it might more
adequately represent the original, which, as Milton himself in-
forms us, is of no certain measure. It may possibly for this rea-
son disappoint the reader, though it cost the writer more labour
than the translation of any other piece in the whole collection.]

STROPHE

My twofold book! single in show,
But double in contents,
Neat, but not curiously adorn'd,
Which, in his early youth,
A poet gave, no lofty one in truth,
Although an earnest wooer of the Muse—
Say while in cool Ausonian shades,
Or British wilds he roam'd,
Striking by turns his native lyre,
By turns the Daunian lute,
And stepp'd almost in air,—

ANTISTROPHE

Say, little book, what furtive hand
Thee from thy fellow-books convey'd,
What time, at the repeated suit
Of my most learned friend,
I sent thee forth, an honour'd traveller,
From our great city to the source of Thames,
Cœrulean sire;
Where rise the fountains, and the raptures ring
Of the Aonian choir,
Durable as yonder spheres,
And through the endless lapse of years
Secure to be admired?

STROPHE II

Now what god, or demigod,
For Britain's ancient genius moved
(If our afflicted land
Have expiated at length the guilty sloth
Of her degenerate sons)
Shall terminate our impious feuds,
And discipline, with hallow'd voice, recall?
Recall the Muses too,
Driven from their ancient seats
In Albion, and well nigh from Albion's shore,
And with keen Phœbean shafts
Piercing the unseemly birds,
Whose talons menace us,
Shall drive the harpy race from Helicon afar?

ANTISTROPHE

But thou, my book, though thou hast stray'd,
Whether by treachery lost,
Or indolent neglect, thy bearer's fault,
From all thy kindred books,
To some dark cell, or cave forlorn,
Where thou endurest, perhaps,
The chafing of some hard untutor'd hand,
Be comforted—
For lo! again the splendid hope appears
That thou may'st yet escape
The gulfs of Lethe, and on oary wings
Mount to the everlasting courts of Jove!

STROPHE III

Since Rouse desires thee, and complains
    That though by promise his,
Thou yet appear'st not in thy place
Among the literary noble stores,
    Given to his care,
But, absent, leavest his numbers incomplete.
    He, therefore, guardian vigilant
    Of that unperishing wealth,
Calls thee to the interior shrine, his charge,
Where he intends a richer treasure far
Than Iön kept (Iön, Erectheus' son
Illustrious, of the fair Creüsa born)
In the resplendent temple of his god,
Tripods of gold, and Delphic gifts divine.

ANTISTROPHE

Haste, then, to the pleasant groves,
    The Muses' favourite haunt;
Resume thy station in Apollo's dome.
    Dearer to him
Than Delos, or the fork'd Parnassian hill!
    Exulting go,
    Since now a splendid lot is also thine,
    And thou art sought by my propitious friend;
    For there thou shalt be read
    With authors of exalted note,
The ancient glorious lights of Greece and Rome.

EPODE

Ye then, my works, no longer vain,
And worthless deem'd by me!
Whate'er this steril genius has produced
Expect, at last, the rage of envy spent,
An unmolested happy home,
Gift of kind Hermes, and my watchful friend;
Where never flippant tongue profane
Shall entrance find,
And whence the coarse unletter'd multitude
Shall babble far remote.
Perhaps some future distant age,
Less tinged with prejudice and better taught,
Shall furnish minds of power
To judge more equally.
Then, malice silenced in the tomb,
Cooler heads and sounder hearts,
Thanks to Rouse, if aught of praise
I merit, shall with candour weigh the claim.

WILLIAM CARTWRIGHT

(1611–1643)

Cartwright was born in Northway, Gloucestershire, before his
family moved to Cirencester (where they kept an inn, not very
successfully). He was educated at Westminster School on a
King's Scholarship. In 1628 he was elected to a Studentship at
Christ Church, Oxford. During his time as an undergraduate he
was apparently the leader of student complaints against disci-
plinary arrangements. In 1636 his play *The Royal Slave* was per-
formed with designs by Inigo Jones and music by Henry
Lawes, during a royal visit to Oxford (and was repeated at
Hampton Court later in 1636). In 1638 he took holy orders;
Wood described him as 'the most florid and seraphical
Preacher' in the University; in 1642 he was appointed Reader in
Metaphysic. In 1643 he died of a fever and was buried in Christ
Church. The King is said to have been moved by the news of his
death. His writings were gathered in the posthumous *Comedies,
Tragi-Comedies, With Other Poems* (1651). His work was much
admired by many of his contemporaries. The verses printed
here relate to the fact that Christ Church, originally known as
Cardinal College and founded by Wolsey, was left only par-
tially built at its founder's fall from power. What is now known
as Tom Quad was built up on only two-and-a-half sides. When
further building was undertaken in the reign of Charles I, it was
again disrupted, this time by the Civil War. (In line 14, 'Quar'
presumably means 'quarry'.)

On The Imperfection of Christ-Church *Buildings*

Arise thou Sacred Heap, and shew a Frame
Perfect at last, and Glorious as thy Name:
Space, and Torn Majesty, as yet are all
Thou hast: we view thy Cradle, as thy Fall.

Our dwelling lyes half desert; The whole space
Unmeeted and unbounded, bears the face
Of the first Ages fields, and we, as they
That stand on hills, have prospect every way:
Like *Theseus* Sonne, curst by Mistake, the frame
Scattred and Torn, hath parts without a Name,
Which in a Landskip some mischance, not meant,
As dropping of the Spunge, would represent;

And (if no succour come) the Time's not far
When 'twill be thought no College, but a Quar.
Send then *Amphion* to these *Thebes* (O Fates)
W'have here as many Breaches, though not gates.
When any Stranger comes, 'tis shewn by us,
As once the face was of *Antigonus*,
With an half-Visage onely: so that all
We boast is but a Kitchin, or an Hall.
Men thence admire, but help not, 't hath the luck
Of Heathen places that were Thunder-strook,
To be ador'd, not toucht; though the Mind and Will
Be in the Pale, the Purse is Pagan still:
Alas th'are Towr's that Thunder do provoke,
We ne'r had Height or Glory for a stroke;
Time, and King *Henry* too, did spare us; we
Stood in those dayes both Sythe, and Scepter-free;
Our Ruines then were licenc'd, and we were
Pass'd by untouch'd, that hand was open here.
Blesse we our Throne then! That which did avoid
The fury of those times, seems yet destroy'd:
So this breath'd on by no full Influence
Hath hung e'r since unminded in suspence,
As doubtfull whether't should Escheated be
To Ruine, or Redeem'd to Majesty.
But great Intents stop seconds, and we owe
To Larger Wants, that Bounty is so slow.
A Lordship here, like *Curtius* might be cast
Into one Hole, and yet not seen at last.
Two sacred Things were thought (by judging souls)
Beyond the Kingdomes Pow'r, *Christchurch* and *Pauls*,
Till, by a Light from Heaven shewn, the one
Did gain his second Renovation,
And some good Star ere long, we do not fear,
Will Guide the Wise to Offer some gifts here.
But Ruines yet stand Ruines, as if none
Durst be so good, as *first to cast a Stone*.
Alas we ask not Prodigies: Wee'd boast
Had we but what is at one Horse-Race lost;
Nor is our House, (as Nature in the fall
Is thought by some) void and bereft of all

But what's new giv'n: Unto our selves we owe
That Sculs are not our Churches Pavement now;
That that's made yet good way; that to his Cup
And *Table Christ* may come, and not ride up;
That no one stumbling fears a worse event,
Nor when he bows falls lower than he meant;
That now our Windows may for Doctrine pass,
And we (as *Paul*) see Mysteries in a *Glass*;
That something elsewhere is perform'd, whereby
'Tis seen we can adorn, though not supply.

But if to all Great Buildings (as to *Troy*)
A God must needs be sent, and we enjoy
No help but Miracle; if so it stand
Decreed by Heav'n, that the same gracious Hand
That perfected our *Statutes*, must be sent
To finish *Christ-Church* too, we are Content;
Knowing that he who in the Mount did give
Those Laws, by which his People were to live,
If they had needed then, as now we do,
Would have bestow'd the *Stone* for *Tables* too.

ABRAHAM COWLEY

(1618–1667)

The seventh and posthumous child of a London stationer, Cowley was educated at Westminster School before entering Trinity College, Cambridge as a Scholar in 1637. He was a Fellow of Trinity from 1640 to 1644, when he was ejected by Parliament on account of his Royalist sympathies. From 1644 to 1645 he lived at St John's College, Oxford, and for ten years thereafter he was with the exiled court in France. He was employed on a range of diplomatic missions, and may also have worked as a spy. On a brief return to London in 1656 he was imprisoned, but soon released on bail. In 1661 he was restored to his fellowship at Trinity. Cowley was writing competent verse by his tenth birthday, and published his first work (*Poetical Blossoms*, 1633) when still only fifteen. He was much admired in his time. Pepys writes thus: 'To my bookseller's and did buy "Scott's Discourse of Witches;" and to hear Mr. Cowley mightily lamented (his death) by Dr. Ward, the Bishop of Winchester, and Dr. Bates, who were standing there, as the best poet of our nation, and as good a man.' His stock has fallen much since then. Cowley also wrote an ode 'Sitting and Drinking in the Chair, made out of the Reliques of Sir Francis Drake's Ship'—an activity no longer encouraged by Bodley's Librarian.

Ode: Mr. Cowley's Book presenting it selfe to the University Library Of Oxford

1

Hail Learnings *Pantheon*! Hail the sacred Ark
Where all the World of Science do's imbarque!
Which ever shall withstand, and hast so long withstood,
  Insatiate Times devouring Flood.
Hail Tree of Knowledg, thy leaves Fruit! which well
Dost in the midst of Paradise arise,
  Oxford the Muses Paradise,
From which may never Sword the blest expell.
Hail Bank of all past Ages! where they lye
T' inrich with interest Posterity!
  Hail Wits Illustrious Galaxy!
Where thousand Lights into one brightness spread;
Hail living University of the Dead!

37

Unconfus'd Babel of all tongues, which er'e
The mighty Linguist Fame, or Time the mighty
    Traveler,
    That could speak, or this could hear.
Majestick Monument and Pyramide,
Where still the shapes of parted Souls abide
Embalm'd in verse, exalted souls which now
Enjoy those Arts they woo'd so well below,
    Which now all wonders plainly see,
    That have been, are, or are to be,
    In the mysterious Library,
The Beatifick *Bodley* of the Deity.

Will you into your Sacred throng admit
    The meanest British Wit?
You Gen'ral Councel of the Priests of Fame,
    Will you not murmur and disdain,
    That I place among you claim,
    The humblest Deacon of her train?
Will you allow me th' honourable chain?
    The chain of Ornament which here
    Your noble Prisoners proudly wear;
A Chain which will more pleasant seem to me
Than all my own Pindarick Liberty:
Will ye to bind me with those mighty names submit,
    Like an Apocrypha with holy Writ?
What ever happy book is chained here,
No other place or People need to fear;
His Chain's a Pasport to go ev'ry where.

As when a seat in Heaven,
Is to an unmalicious Sinner given,
　Who casting round his wondring eye,
Does none but Patriarchs and Apostles there espye;
　Martyrs who did their lives bestow,
　And Saints who Martyrs liv'd below;
With trembling and amazement he begins,
To recollect his frailties past and sins,
　He doubts almost his Station there,
His soul sayes to it self, How came I here?
It fares no otherwise with me
When I my self with conscious wonder see,
Amidst this purifi'd elected Companie.
　With hardship they, and pain,
　Did to this happiness attain:
No labour I, nor merits can pretend,
I think Predestination only was my friend.

Ah, that my Authour had been ty'd like me
To such a place, and such a Companie!
Instead of sev'ral Countries, sev'ral Men,
　And business which the Muses hate,
He might have then improv'd that small Estate,
Which nature sparingly did to him give,
　He might perhaps have thriven then,
And setled, upon me his Child, somewhat to live.
'T had happier been for him, as well as me,
　For when all, (alas) is done,
We Books, I mean, You Books, will prove to be
The best and noblest conversation.
　For though some errors will get in,
　Like Tinctures of Original sin:
　Yet sure we from our Fathers wit
　Draw all the strength and Spirit of it:
Leaving the grosser parts for conversation,
As the best blood of Man's imploy'd in generation.

Upon the Chair made out of Sir Francis Drakes *Ship,*
presented to the University Library in Oxford, *by* John
Davis *of* Deptford, *Esquire*

To this great Ship which round the Globe has run,
And matcht in Race the Chariot of the Sun,
This *Pythagorean* Ship (for it may claim
Without presumption so deserv'd a Name,
By knowledge once and transformation now)
In her New Shape this sacred Port allow.
Drake and his Ship could not have wish'd from Fate,
A more blest Station, or more blest Estate.
For (Lo!) a Seat of endless Rest is given,
To her in *Oxford*, and to him in Heaven.

MARTIN LLUELYN

(1616–1682)

Lluelyn was born in London of a Welsh family. Educated at Westminster School, he followed the well-trodden path to Christ Church, matriculating in 1636. Having been made a Student, he was ejected by the Parliamentary Visitors in 1648, and took up work in London as a physician. He was awarded his MD from Oxford in 1653 and became a Fellow of the College of Physicians in 1659. He wrote congratulatory verses to Charles at the Restoration, and was made Physician Extraordinary to the King. In 1660 he was appointed Principal of St Mary Hall in Oxford. In 1661 a play of his composition was performed on the occasion of a royal visit to Oxford. In 1664 he moved to High Wycombe, continuing his work as a physician. He became Mayor of High Wycombe in 1671.

from *A Curse to Vulcan, Occasioned by a Great Fire in Oxford, which began at the Rosting of a Pigge 1643*

Pox take you, *Vulcan*, & may that curse spread
All the *Pye-Corner* curses on thy head:
What? not a *Pigge* the Parsons *Venson* drest,
But needs your Cuckoldship must be a Guest,
And make the same Dish without more adoe,
Rosted and *smoakt* be Pigge and Bacon too?
Shame on your foule *West phalia* teeth, for me,
Your next Pigge shall be *souc't* with a vengance t'ye.
Some *Houshould* cause sure made you visit us,
Tis for the *Wives* sake you love *Swines* flesh thus,
For her Tyth Vrchin *Cupid* without doubt,
Was *Litterd Pigge*, and his eyes *Rosted* out.
Time was, ere your so furious Rites did rise,
A penny-Faggot was a Sacrifice.
Some heard your Engine *Browne*, the Woodman say
Six Billets cloyd you on a Gawdy day.

But now those lofty Piles which lately stood,
The pride of *Shot-over*, and *Bagley Wood*,
Are *By-Repast*, and *homely* Diet growne;
Nought can allay *your* Fury, but a *Towne*.
Well give me but your *Tosted* fist a while,
And I shall shew you in this Ruind Pile,
(Like him that showes the *Tombes*, and's own Nose
    where
Those *Graves* and *Dust* are now, and whose they were.
You din'd Hell doe you good on't, at the *Pigge*,
Which sure was *Rosted* well, were't nere so *bigge*.
But not content to feed as you could catch,
On so *course* Meat as *Hospitable* Thatch,
You foam'd and chaf'd, tasted the *Barnes*, and *Hay*,
And swallowed all the *Wood yards* in the Way.
And then you and your warme Tempestuous Trayne,
Followd by sent into a close *by-Lane*.   [Note: New Inne Lane.]
Where you had seiz'd the Mint, but that withall
Aurum Potabile was too Cordiall.
Where you had injur'd those by Rash
    designe   [Note: Sir W.P. his Quarter.]
Whom virtue more then all thy *Flame* Refines.
But Fire's a *Glutton*, *Vulcan*, all the Rest
Did but *provoke*, the *Shambles* were your *Feast*.
Here while you Rove about and Wanton runne,
Flesh was your *Fuell* and Provision.
Here you fell on amaine, and fed as hard,
As you had been a *Gyant* o'the *Guard*.
Entrailes and *Skinnes* goe to't, and All you eate,
The *Stalles* and *Beeves*, the *Trenchers*, and the *Meate*.
Buildings on either hand submit their height,
While Flame consumes what did support their Weight.
And here an *Honest Loyall* Printer   [Note: L.L. Pr. to the Univers:]
    dwelt,
Who all the Furie of the Tempest felt,
One that had never yet deserv'd these Fires,
By trying how *well* Treason looks in *Quires*.
Nor Printing *Votes*, where letters *forward* lye,
But must be read still with an Hebrew Eye.
Where Truths *runne Counter*, that which way they goe,

42

Rabbines and *Sea Crabs* which goe backward, know.
He to cast *Ordnance* was still afraid,
Bell-Mettle Letters he us'd none in's Trade.
Nor *desperate* Orders ever did he dresse,
Where *Inke* and *Conscience* are both ith' Presse.
That when the Worke is ore 'tis hard to state
If *booke* or *Printer* should be stitcht up straight . . .

ROBERT HEATH

(1620–1697)

Heath was born at Brested in Kent. He was admitted to Corpus
Christi College, Cambridge, in 1634 but left the following year
(his father was also dismissed from his position as Chief Justice
of the Court of Common Pleas in 1635—the two events were
probably not unconnected). He fought with Prince Rupert in
the Civil War, was captured in 1645, but escaped and took part
in both the battle of Naseby and the siege of Oxford (presum-
ably the occasion of the poem below). He went into exile on the
Continent, returning around 1651. He worked as a barrister be-
fore retiring to Kent, where he died. In addition to the miscella-
neous poems in *Clarastella*, he left a manuscript translation of
the *Aeneid* (now in the William Andrews Clark Library in the
University of California) which remains unpublished.

On the Creeple Souldiers Marching in Oxford *in the Lord* Thr. Cottington's *Companie*

Stay Gentlemen! and you shal see a very rare sight;
Souldiers who though they want arms, yet wil fight:
Nay some of them have never a leg but onely *Will*:
Their Governour, and yet they'l stand to it stil.
The birds call'd *Apodes* they resemble, and seem
To be without either wing or leg, like them.
Oh the courage of a drunken and valiant man!
For each wil be going when he cannot stand!
Then room for Criples! here comes a companie,
Such as before I think you ne'r did see:
Here's one like a Pidgion goes pinion'd in spight
Of old *Priapus*, the birds to affright:
Another limps as if he had got the Pharse,
With his half leg like a Goose close up to his arse.
Yet mistake me not! this is no Puppet play;
You shal onely see the several motions to day.
Ran: tan: tan: with a spanish march and gate

44

Thus they follow their Leader according to his wonted
    state.
A Snaile or a Crablouse would march in a day.
If driven as led with the white staffe as far as they,
What I should cal them I hardly do know,
Foot they are not as appears by the show:
By the wearing of their Musquets to which they are ty'd,
They should be Dragooners had they horses to ride.
And yet now I think on't, they cannot be suc;
Because each man hath his rest for his crutch,
To these their Officer need not to say at alar'ms,
Stand to your Colours, or handle your arms:
Yet that they are Souldiours, you safely may say,
For they'l die before they wil run away:
Nay, they are stout as ever were *Vantrumps*,
For like *Widdrington* they'l fight upon their very stumps.
They have keen Estridge stomacks, and wel disgest
Both Iron and Lead, as a Dog wil a breast
Of Mutton. But now to their Pedigree;
That they are sons of *Mars*, most writers agree;
Some conceive from the Badger old *Vulcan* they came,
Because like him they are Mettle-men and lame,
The moderns think they came from the *Guyes of Warwick*;
    and
Some think they are of the old *Herculean* band:
For as by his foot he was discover'd, so
By their feet you their valour may know.
And though many wear wooden legs and crutches,
Yet, by *Hercules*, I can assure you, such is
Their steeled resolution, that here
You'l find none that wil the woodden dagger wear.
They're true and trustie *Trojans* all believe me,
And stride their wooden Palfreis well: t'would grieve
    me
To see them tire before they get
Unto the Holy-bush; but yet
If they should faint, at that end of the town,
    They may set up their horses and lie down.
    Most of these fighters, I would have you to know,
    Were our brave *Edgehil Mermidons* awhile agoe.

45

Who were their limbs like their looser rags
Ready to leave them at the next hedge, with brags,
That through the merit of their former harms,
They die like Gentlemen though they bear no arms.

Now some wil suspect that my Muse may be,
'Cause she is so lame, of this Companie:
And the rather, because one verse sometimes,
Is much shorter then his fellows to hold up the rithmes;
I confess before Criples to halt is not good:
Yet for excuse shee pleads, she understood
That things by their similies are best displaid,
And for that cause her feet are now Iambick made.

HENRY VAUGHAN
(1622–1695)

Born at Newton-by-Usk, in Breconshire, Vaughan was pri-
vately educated (with his twin brother Thomas) at Llangattock,
before matriculating at Jesus College, Oxford, in 1638. He ap-
pears not to have taken a degree, but later studied law and
medicine. He served in the Royalist company led by Colonel
Price, and practised medicine near his birthplace, from 1645
until his death. In his literary work he styled himself a 'Silurist'
in reference to the Silures, an ancient people of South Wales.
The visionary poems of *Silex Scintillans* (1650, 1655) remain en-
duringly powerful.

On Sir Thomas Bodley's Library; the Author being then in Oxford

Boast not proud *Golgotha*: that thou can'st show
The ruines of mankind, and let us know
How fraile a thing is flesh! though we see there
But empty Skulls, the *Rabbins* still live here.
They are not dead, but full of *Blood* again,
I mean the *Sense*, and ev'ry *Line* a *Vein*.
Triumph not o're their Dust; whoever looks
In here, shall find their *Brains* all in their Books.
Nor is't old *Palestine* alone survives,
Athens lives here, more than in *Plutarch*'s lives.
The stones which sometimes danc'd unto the strain
Of *Orpheus*, here do lodge his muse again.
And you the *Roman* Spirits, learning has
Made your lives longer, than your Empire was.
Cœsar had perish'd from the World of men,
Had not his *Sword* been rescu'd by his *pen*.
Rare *Seneca*! how lasting is thy breath?
Though Nero did, thou could'st not bleed to Death.
How dull the expert Tyrant was, to look
For that in thee, which lived in thy Book?
Afflictions turn our *Blood* to *Ink*, and we
Commence when *Writing*, our *Eternity*.
Lucilius here I can behold, and see
His *Counsels* and his *Life* proceed from thee.

47

But what care I to whom thy *Letters* be?
I change the *Name*, and thou do'st write to me;
And in this Age, as sad almost as thine,
Thy stately *Consolations* are mine.
Poor Earth! what though thy viler dust enrouls
The frail Inclosures of these mighty Souls?
Their graves are all upon Record; not one
But is as bright, and open as the Sun.
And though some part of them obscurely fell
And perish'd in an unknown, private Cell:
Yet in their books they found a glorious way
To live unto the Resurrection-day.
Most noble *Bodley*! we are bound to thee
For no small part of our *Eternity*.
Thy treasure was not spent on *Horse* and *Hound*,
Nor that new Mode, which doth old *States* confound.
Thy legacies another way did go:
Nor were they left to those would spend them so.
Thy safe, discreet Expence on us did flow;
Walsam is in the mid'st of *Oxford* now.
Th' hast made us all thine *Heirs*: whatever we
Hereafter write, 'tis thy *Posterity*.
This is thy *Monument*! here thou shalt stand
Till the times fail in their last grain of Sand.
And wheresoe're thy silent *Reliques* keep,
This *Tomb* will never let thine honour sleep.
Still we shall think upon thee; all our fame
Meets here to speak one *Letter* of thy name.
Thou can'st not dye! here thou art more than safe
Where every *Book* is thy large *Epitaph*.

HENRY BOLD

(1627–1683)

Bold was born in Hampshire and educated at Winchester College. In 1645 he was made a Fellow of New College, a position from which he was ejected by the Parliamentary Visitors in 1648. Thereafter he lived in London, working in the Examiner's Office in Chancery Lane. His earliest publication, *Wit a sporting in a Pleasant Grove of New Fancies*, appeared in 1657; his last, *Latine Songs with their English and Poems*, posthumously in 1685. Some of his poetry plagiarizes that of Herrick and other contemporaries.

On the first sight of the Lady M. W. *in* St. Maries *Church* Oxon.

Pox take this *learning*! burn these *books*
There's a Ladies powerful looks
Draw, my *Thoughts* to fix upon,
Her *Divine perfection*:
    Whose *bright Eyes* do guild the *day*
    Whilest *enlighten'd*, by your *Ray*
    Love can *flie* no other *way*.

When from the *Temple's sacred shine*
She did glance *her Eyes*, on *mine*,
Cupid *there*, did *light* his *Dart*,
To *enflame* my *Tender heart*:
    Pulpit *Thunder* could not move,
    Eyes, or *thoughts*, resolved to prove,
    No *Religion sweet*, but *Love*.

While my *senses* here do *Jarre*,
Love contrives a double Warre,
Through mine *Eyes*, he throwes his *Dart*,
Through mine *Ears*, assaults my *Heart*
    So this *Angel*, charm'd mine *Eare*,
    With her *Singing*, that I swear,
    Those *above* might *rival* her.

But alas! Those *Suns* are gone!
And that *Heavenly musick* done!

Yet return *those murthering Eyes,*
To behold your *Sacrifice!*
    Nor, think I, thou *joy'st* to see
    Love-*sick-Souls* should *die* for *thee*:
    But, to *Sweeten death* for *me.*

Or if that *Lady,* in whose *Breast,*
My fled *Heart,* is lodg'd a *Guest,*
Will *Exchange* (but Oh! I fear
Her's, is stray'd, some other where)
    I may *Live;* if not; I *dye,*
    Martyr, to her *Diety,*
    To encrease, her *Victory.*

Her a brown *Hair,* a *snare* might prove,
To entangle captive *Jove:*
In the *Circles* of her *Eye,*
Cupids fetter'd *Rebels* lye:
    Would'st thou know, *who this* might be
    That hath *stolne,* my *Heart,* from me?
    These few *marks* will say, tis she.

At the Surrender of Oxon.

Thou *Man of Men,* who e're *thou* art,
That hast a *Loyal, Royal Heart,*
Despaire not! though thy *Fortune* frown!
Our *Cause,* is Gods, and not our *Own;*
'Twere *sin,* to harbour *Jealous feares,*
The *World* laments, for *Cavaleers, Cavaleers.*

Those *Things* (like *Men*) that swarm, ith' *Town,*
Like *Motions,* wander up, and down;
And were the *Rogues,* not full of *blood,*
You'd swear, *they men* were, made of *wood:*
The *Fellow-feeling-wanton* swears,
There are no *Men,* but *Cavaleers, &c.*

Ladies, be *pearl*, their *Diamond Eyes*,
And curse, *Dame Shipton's Prophecyes*
Fearing they never shall be sped,
To *wrestle*, for a *Maiden-head*:
But *feelingly*, with doleful tears,
They *sigh*, and *mourn* for *Cavaleers, &c.*

Our grave *Divines*, are *silenc'd* quite.
Ecclipsing thus, our *Churches Light*:
Religion's made a *mock*, and all
Good *wayes*, as *Works*, *Apocryphal*:
Our *Gallants* baffel'd, *slaves* made *Peers*,
While *Oxford*, weeps for *Cavaleers, &c.*

Townsmen complain, they are *undone*,
Their *Fortunes* faile, and *all* is *gone*,
Rope *makers*, only *live* in *hopes*,
To have good *trading*, for their *Ropes*,
And *Glovers* thrive, by *Round-heads Ears*,
When *Charles* returns, with's *Cavaleers, Cavaleers.*

JOHN DRYDEN

(1631–1700)

One of many poets educated at Westminster School, Dryden was an undergraduate at Trinity College, Cambridge. He built himself a literary career in London, and produced an enormous output (most of it of an astonishingly high standard) of poetry, drama, and criticism. His work as a verse translator ranks him very highly among English exponents of that demanding art. Often involved in political and literary controversies, he was appointed Poet Laureate in 1668 and Historiographer Royal in 1670—posts he held until the Revolution of 1688. His works include a number of theatrical prologues written for performances in Oxford—the one below being for an unspecified play. Another prologue, 'Spoken by Mr. Hart, at the Acting of the *Silent Woman*', observes (with polite flattery) that 'Poetry, which is in *Oxford* made / An Art, in *London* onely is a Trade.' Few in the history of English poetry have pursued that 'trade' more assiduously than Dryden.

Prologue to the University of Oxford

Tho' Actors cannot much of Learning boast,
Of all who want it, we admire it most.
We love the Praises of a Learned Pit,
As we remotely are ally'd to Wit.
We speak our Poets Wit, and Trade in Ore,
Like those who touch upon the Golden Shore:
Betwixt our Judges can distinction make,
Discern how much, and why, our Poems take.
Mark if the Fools, or Men of Sence, rejoyce,
Whether th' applause be only Sound or Voice.
When our Fop Gallants, or our City Folly
Clap over-loud, it makes us melancholy:
We doubt that Scene which does their wonder raise,
And, for their ignorance contemn their Praise.
Judge then, if We who Act, and They who Write,
Shou'd not be proud of giving You delight.
London likes grossly, but this nicer Pit
Examines, Fathoms all the depths of Wit:
The ready Finger lays on every Blot,

Knows what shou'd justly please, and what shou'd not.
Nature her self lies open to your view,
You judge by Her what draught of Her is true,
Where out lines false, and Colours seem too faint,
Where Bunglers dawb, and where True Poets Paint.
But by the Sacred Genius of this Place,
By every Muse, by each Domestick Grace,
Be kind to Wit, which but endeavours well,
And, where you judge, presumes not to excel.
Our Poets hither for Adoption come,
As Nations su'd to be made Free of *Rome*.
Not in the suffragating Tribes to stand,
But in your utmost, last, Provincial Band.
If His Ambition may those Hopes pursue,
Who with Religion loves Your arts and You,
Oxford to Him a dearer Name shall be,
Than His own Mother University.
Thebes did his Green, unknowing Youth ingage,
He chuses *Athens* in His Riper Age.

HENRY ALDRICH

(1647–1710)

Educated at Westminster School, Aldrich entered Christ
Church in 1662; he became a Canon in 1682 and Dean in 1689.
He designed the college's Peckwater Quadrangle; he distin-
guished himself as an anti-Catholic controversialist in works
such as *A Reply to Two Discourses Concerning the Adoration of Our
Blessed Saviour in the Holy Eucharist* (1687). His *Artis Logicæ Com-
pendium* (1692) was frequently reissued. He was an amateur
composer of songs and catches. (The words of this catch were
attributed to Henry Bold in his posthumous *Latine Songs* of
1685.)

Oh the merry *Christ-Church* Bells,
One, two, three four, five, six,
They are so woundy great,
So wondrous sweet
And they trowl so merrily, merrily.
Oh the first and second Bell
That every day at four and ten
Cries come come, come come, come to Prayers,
And the Verger troops before the Dean.
Tingle, Tingle, Ting, goes the small bell at nine
To call the Beerers home,
But there's never a man
Will leave his can,
Till he hears the mighty Tom.

RICHARD LEIGH
(1649?–1728)

Leigh came from a propertied family whose main home was Rushall Hall, near Walsall. He matriculated at Queen's College, Oxford, in 1666 and took his BA in 1669. Wood says that he then became an actor, but there is no evidence to support this, and it seems unlikely. Certainly he later became a doctor, and at the time of his death he was described as 'M.D. of Wolverhampton'. His earliest publication was *The Censure of the Rota on Mr. Dryden's Conquest of Granada* (1673) which involved him in a miniature pamphlet war—Dryden labelled him 'the Fastidious Brisk of Oxford'. In the same year he published the *Transposer Rehearsed*, a contribution to the dispute between Parker (supported by Leigh) and Marvell. His sole collection of *Poems* was published in 1675, and, though uneven, contains some fine lyrics. The Sheldonian Theatre was opened on 9 July, 1669.

On the Oxford Theater

Those glorious *Heights* which *Art* of old did raise,
Liv'd uncommended in their own first *Days.*
While yet their *Pinnacles* did *newly* rise,
And they possest a *new place* in the *Skies;*
The *gazing Eyes* of all they on them drew,
Admiring slowly what as *slowly grew.*
Their *Fame* they spread by being longer known,
And growing older, doubled their *Renown*:
This goodly *Pile,* born in the *present Age,*
The *Pens* of *after-Poets* shall ingage,
Making their *Verse* immortal with its *Praise,*
The *Argument* their *Crown,* and *Theme* their *Bayes.*

The *silent Muses,* conscious of their shame,
Urge their *Amazement* to excuse the blame.
They in *astonishment* and *wonder* lost,
No more the glory of their *Numbers* boast.
For what above the *height* of *Verse* does *rise,*
And with best *Poets Lines* for *lasting* vies,
Requires no *Muse* to celebrate its Name
It self does best to all it self proclaim.

Its *Eloquence* their *Silence* does excuse,
Poet it self, and to itself a *Muse*.
A various Fate commuting each *Extreme*,
Theaters *speak*, while Poets *Statues* seem.

Greatness, as its due, this Respect may claim,
Due to the *Fabrick*'s and the *Founder*'s Fame;
That *this Age* should not hastily presume
To *write*, what *Story* is of *all to come*.
But when the *Interval* of *Wonder*'s past,
And the *Amusement* does no longer last;
This *Theater* that makes *our Age* admire,
Succeeding ones shall in it's *Praise* inspire.

But had the beauteous *Frame* been rear'd of old,
What *Divine Tales* the *Wits* had of it told!
Then had we heard, how some *Amphion* plaid,
And toucht those *Strings* which the *Foundations* laid.
While dancing *Stones* which did in *Measures* close,
To various *Sounds*, in various *Figures* rose;
Advancing still in comely *Ranks*, till all
Did into *Order* and *Proportion* fall.
Their *Fairy Seats* they had from this deriv'd,
And all their *Scenes* of *Bliss* like this contriv'd.
This then had been, though with another name,
The *Palace* of the *Sun* and *House* of *Fame*.
Ovid had built, and shining *Pillars* plac't,
Where *Virgil*'s Hand had rich plain *Figures* cast.
Th' *Egyptian* Kings that with *Embalmings* kept,
Long uncorrupted in their *Marbles* slept,
Their *Royal Bodies* in their Tombs *inthron'd*
With greater Pomp, than others have been *Crown'd*:
Though *Living*, they less nobly dwelt than *Dead*;
Had here, their *crowned Heads* more richly laid.
This had been number'd with the blest Abodes
Of *Oracles*, and Dwellings of the *Gods*.
This with their *Shrines* and *Monuments* had vy'd:
Gods here had *liv'd*, and *Princes* here had *dy'd*.

This to the *Work*. But what should all erect
In honour of so wise an *Architect*?
Who th' *Image* yet *unborn* did entertain,
And hous'd the *Theater* within his *Brain*.
There once *it stood*, so great, so strong, so fair,
And so adorn'd; as now it does appear.
Each *Part* its *measure, use* and *place* possest,
Without the least encroachment on the *rest*.
Distinct, as *Platonists* those *Beauties* feign'd,
Which in *Idea*'s their *First Mind* contein'd.
The *Intellectual Theater* appear'd,
As in the *Fancy* by a *Builder* rear'd.
And labour'd with less *noise*, but not less *Art*
Than that, to which it *Pattern* did impart.

What is the *Founder*'s due? whose brave *Soul* gives
As largely as the *Artists hand* contrives.
A *Soul*, like his Skill, *vast*, like his Work, *great*;
Capacious though that be, of *more Receit*.
If that for *hugest Crowds* does *place* provide,
This *more receives*, and *opens* yet *more wide*.
So *full* of *Room*, and of so *free Access*,
As neither *Straitness* knows, nor *Emptiness*.
Many such *Theaters* lodge in that *Breast*,
Where *this* at largest, a *small space* possest.

Such as of old their Courage did employ
To root out *Monsters*, or their *Foes* destroy;
Who sav'd their *Countrey* from the *Lions Den*,
Or from such *Wolves*, as *Men* were then to *Men*:
But *Heroes* were, and triumph'd in the Field.
They were their *Gods*, that taught them how to *Build*.
Who *new Worlds* discover'd, Fame less renowns,
Than who the *old World* vary'd with *new Towns*.
If *Bacchus* for one *India* found, had praise,
A *Pair* of *Gods* the Walls of *Troy* did raise.
Who Empires Bounds with *Conquests* did enlarge,
Or with *Plantations* farther off, orecharge,
Did add, to what already was too vast,
Who *Built*, adorn'd and beautify'd the *Wast*.

Thus *Nature* one World, *Art* another made,
Or else the Old World with a New inlaid.
Art with her *People* too, her *World* did grace,
With carv'd *Colonies*, and a Marble *Race*.
The num'rous *Off-springs* of a fertile *Line*
In long *Successions* did of *Statues* shine.
And to the younger Ages then were shown
Their *dead* Forefathers *living shapes* in Stone.

A *Pillar* or *Coloss*, preserv'd their Fame,
Their *Images* did half their Honours claim.
Nor did alas! *Inscriptions* always speak
The noble *Roman*, or the gallant *Greek*.
How many *Stones*, whose *Titles* now defac'd,
(*Time* carving *new Marks* to supply the *rased*.)
Attend this *Fabrick*, and at distance wait,
Expecting yet with it, a braver Fate?
Others but from their *Monuments* derive
That *Name*, which SHELDON to his *Pile* shall give.
Maintain'd by *that*, as by the Builders *hand*,
It long as *Time*, firm as *Himself* shall stand;
And Structures yet *unborn* as much out-last,
As it in Height transcends all Buildings *past*.

THOMAS FLATMAN

(1637–1688)

The son of a clerk in Chancery, Flatman became a Scholar of New College in 1654, but left three years later without taking a degree. After some time in Cambridge, he lived and worked in London as a miniature painter. He was made a Fellow of the Royal Society in 1668. His work as a miniaturist, such as his *Self-Portrait* of 1673, now in the Victoria and Albert Museum, has generally received more praise than his poetry. He died in Three-Leg Alley, St Brides, in 1688. Samuel Austin was a Cornishman who had a high regard for his own poetic abilities. Wood describes him as 'a conceited coxcomb'. A group of ironic 'admirers' obtained copies of his work and published a selection as *Naps upon Parnassus. A sleepy Muse nipt and pinch't, though not awakened* in 1658, prefacing it with more than twenty mock encomia, including Flatman's. (The 'Bongraces' of line 27 are broad-rimmed hats.)

To Mr. Sam. Austin of Wadham Col. Oxon, on his Most Unintelligible Poems

In that small inch of time I stole, to look
On th' obscure depths of your mysterious Book,
(Heav'n bless my eye-sight!) what strains did I see?
What Steropegeretick Poetrie!
What Hieroglyphick words, what all,
In Letters more than Cabalistical!
We with our fingers may your Verses scan,
But all our Noddles understand them can
No more, than read that dung fork, pothook hand
That in *Queen's Colledge Library* does stand.
The cutting Hanger of your wit I can't see,
For that same scabbard that conceals your Fancy:
Thus a black velvet Casket hides a Jewel;
And a dark woodhouse, wholesom winter fuel;
Thus *John Tradeskin* starves our greedy eyes,
By boxing up his new-found Rarities;

We dread *Actæons* Fate, dare not look on,
When you do scowre your skin in *Helicon*;
We cannot *(Lynceus*-like) see through the wall
Of your strong-Morter'd *Poems*; nor can all
The small shot of our Brains make one hole in
The Bulwark of your Book, that Fort to win.
Open your meanings door, O do not lock it!
Undo the Buttons of your smaller Pocket,
And charitably spend those Angels there,
Let them inrich and actuate our sphere.
Take off our Bongraces, and shine upon us,
Though your resplendent beams should chance to tan
    us.
Had you but stoln your Verses, then we might
Hope in good time they would have come to light;
And felt I not a strange Poetick heat
Flaming within, which reading makes me sweat,
Vulcan should take 'em, and I'd not exempt 'em,
Because they're things *Quibus lumen ademptum*.
I thought to have commended something there,
But all exceeds my commendations far,
I can say nothing; but stand still, and stare,
And cry, O wondrous, strange, profound, & rare.
Vast Wits must fathom you better than thus.
You merit more than their praise: as for us
    The Beetles of our Rhimes shall drive full fast in,
    The wedges of your worth to everlasting,
    My Much *Apocalyptiqu'* friend *Sam. Austin*.

TOM BROWN
(1663–1704)

Brown was born in Shropshire. It was while an undergraduate at Christ Church (which he entered in 1678) that he wrote his adaptation of one of Martial's epigrams (I.32) 'Non amo te, Sabidi', supposedly when under threat of expulsion by Dr John Fell, distinguished Dean of Christ Church and Royal Chaplain. Brown left Oxford without a degree, and after a spell as a teacher at Kingston-on-Thames, he settled in London as a hack writer, producing many translations (from Erasmus, Scarron, Petronius, Lucian, and others) as well as satirical pamphlets and poems, many of them as contributions to feuds with Dryden, Blackmore, and others. His account of London life in *Amusements Serious and Comical, Calculated for the Meridian of London* (1700) remains entertaining. A two-volume set of his *Works* was published in 1707. (Brown's version from Martial, as printed here, has undergone many small changes in its later transmission.)

> I do not love thee, Dr. Fell,
> But why I cannot tell;
> But this I know full well,
> I do not love thee, Dr. Fell.

JOHN GLANVIL

(1664?–1735)

The grandson of Sir John Glanvil, Speaker of Parliament, Glanvil became a commoner of Trinity College in 1678 and a Scholar two years later. He tried for a fellowship at All Souls, but was defeated by Thomas Creech. His habitual drunkenness apparently prevented his obtaining a fellowship at Trinity. His publications included entertaining imitations of Horace (*Some Odes of Horace imitated with relation to his Majesty and the Times* (1690)), the first English translation of Fontenelle's *A Plurality of Worlds* (1688) and—probably—a pastoral elegy on Purcell (Damon (1696)).

A Drinking Song. Occasioned by an Auction at Oxford, in the year 1685, or 1686.

I

> Let the provident Fop
> For an Author bid up,
> 'Till the critical Half-penny carry't;
> Secure he may be,
> And unrival'd for me,
> Unless 'twere an Auction of Claret.

II

> Were Champaign but expos'd,
> I'd vy with the most,
> But for useless Books, let them rot all;
> What the Devil care I
> Who'll *Bellarmine* buy,
> Give me but a *Bellarmine* Bottle?

III

> Each Glass of good Wine
> Excells the best Line
> Of the Learned, the Wise, or the Godly;
> Each Bottle we count
> To a Tome does amount,
> And a Cellar's worth more than a *Bodley*.

IV

With Cost, and with Pain
We dull Learning obtain;
At cheapest 'tis damnable hard Gain;
While the Wine we adore,
Enlightens us more,
And Pleasure gives into the Bargain.

V

Then about with your Wine,
If for Wit you design;
Fair Drinking's the Way to acquire it.
The fam'd God of Wit
To the Name has no Right,
But by rip'ning the Grape to inspire it.

ALICIA D'ANVERS

(1668?–1725)

Alicia D'Anvers was, according to Anthony à Wood, the daughter of Samuel Clarke, who was director of printing in the University of Oxford and a man learned in several languages, including Persian and Hebrew. His daughter Alicia married Knightley Danvers at an unknown date before December 1690. In 1691 she published dutiful (and dull) verses dedicated to Queen Mary (*A Poem upon His Sacred Majesty . . .*), in praise of William. In the same year she published the altogether livelier *Academia: Or the Humours of the University of Oxford*, in part narrated in the persona of a male servant and offering a witty account of the follies (and worse) of the University. Two years later, D'Anvers also published *The Oxford-Act: A Poem*, a burlesque account of University ceremonial. ('Hed—tons' in line 28 is an abbreviation of Headington's, referring to what was then a village just outside Oxford.)

from *Academia*

When they've been there about a *Quarter*,
Say half a *Year*, or such a matter,
Their *Friends* think it more orderly
To send their *Mony* quarterly;
By this time, they have more occasion
For *Ready*, than the poor o'th *Nation*,
Thinking they know better the use on't,
A *Peer* o'th *Realm* is less profuse on't;
That *Week* o'th *Quarter*, as they have it,
He's damned with *them* who thinks to save it:
Now for that *necessary Trick*,
To *book*, and *score*, and *run a Tick*,
For *Gown*, and *Cap*, for *Drink*, and *Smoke*,
And so much more for *Ink*, and *Chalk*;
Five pounds a *Coat*,—*Ink* Five more—Ten,
Six bottles,—*Chalk* as much agen;
A *Glass* broke, *Six pence*—so much more,
Because 'twas put upon the *Score*.
And at this rate the *Coxcombs* run
Their *Daddies* out of *House* and Home;

Those that in *Debt*, the least may be,
Perhaps owe Hundreds two, or three,
Till fallen downright *sick* of Duns,
Keeps Chamber, till the *Carrier* comes;
The *ready Mony*, when they send it,
He must upon his *Mistress* spend it;
And so that very *Night* he runs
To honest *Joan* of Hed—tons,
Who brags she has been a *Beginner*
With many an after-hardened *Sinner*;
As to a *Book* an *Introduction's*
To *Vice*, so she, and her *Instruction's*. . .
And now no question, but you'l ask
How 'tis, they so neglect their Task,
Folks can't do all at once, for look, Sir,
They've more to do than con a Book, sure,
For *Sundays* work, it very fare is,
To see, who preaches at St. *Maries*,
Peep in at *Carfax Church*, to see there,
Either who preaches, or what *she there*:
Then, as if troubled with the *Squitters*,
Away they feque it to, St. *Peters*,
When up into the *Chancel* coming,
Which most an end is full of *Women*,
About they strut a while, and seek out,
And one vouchsafe at last, to pick out,
Or say; *pox, ne'ere a handsome Woman* . . .
Always when once 'tis Afternoon,
Duns with the *Colleges* have done;
And Scholars *looking well about*,
With caution, venture to go out;
For many times it happens s'os,
I'th very face *to meet their foes*:
With Sir, *you know you owe me, for*
Maintaining of *your Spotted Cur*;

I'm sure, I bought him as good *Meat*,
As any *Christian*, Sir, *could eat*:
If there's in Man any Belief,
I always fed the Whelp with Beef;
A deal of Money, *I disburst so,*
And *Money* going out of *Purse so*—
I'd ask'd your *Tutor*, but to stay me,
You said, that you'd next *Quarter pay me,*
'Las I'me a *poor Man*, that you know,
And yet you'l *never pay me too.*
The *Sparks so thunder-struck at this,*
He hardly can tell what he is,
Protests to *Harry*, he is willing
To pay, bids him, *here*, *take that shilling,*
Being all he has now in his Pocket,
As for his Chest he can't unlock it,
Because he has either spoil'd his *Key,*
Lost it, or laid it out o'th'way;
And says, when e're he comes for the rest,
He'll pay him, or he'll *break his Chest.*
These words give *Harry* Satisfaction
Beyonde th'event, or *threaten'd Action;*
Who fancies in this *Chest a Mint,*
When there is ne'ere a penny in't . . .

ABEL EVANS

(1679–1737)

Evans was educated at Merchant Taylors' School before entering St John's College, Oxford, in 1692. He took holy orders in 1700 and held a series of incumbencies, including St Giles, Oxford. He had a turbulent career as Chaplain of St John's, at one time being dismissed for making a public speech criticizing the College president. Well-known as a wit and epigrammatist and as a good preacher, he was described by one contemporary as a 'loose, ranting gentleman'. He is the subject of an anonymous contemporary epigram:

On Dr. Evans Cutting Down a Row of Trees at St. John's College, Oxford

Indulgent Nature on each kind bestows
A secret instinct to discern its foes:
The goose, a silly bird, avoids the fox;
Lambs fly from wolves; and sailors steer from rocks.
Evans, the gallows as his fate foresees,
And bears the like antipathy to trees.

Evans corresponded with Pope and is favourably mentioned in Book II of *The Dunciad*. The 'Danby' of *Vertumnus* (the poem takes its title from the Roman divinity of the same name, the god of seasonal transformation in general, and of the transformations of plants in particular) is Henry Danvers, Earl of Danby (1573–1644) who, in 1621 leased from Magdalen College the land on which the Oxford Physic Garden (now the Botanic Garden) was established; he is commemorated in the name of the main gate to the Garden. Jacob Bobart the younger (1641–1719) succeeded his father as Superintendent of the Garden and was for some time Botanical Professor in the University.

from *Vertumnus*

On *Isis* Banks, Retirement sweet!
Tritonian *Pallas* holds her Seat . . .
Minerva's Gardens are Thy Care;
JACOB, the Goddess Maid revere.
All *Plants* which *Europe*'s fields contain;
For Health, for Pleasure, or for Pain:
(From the tall Cedar, that does rise
With Conic Pride and mates the Skies;
Down to the humblest Shrub that crawls
On Earth, or just ascends our Walls,)
Her Squares of Horticulture yield:
By *DANBY* Planted, *BOBART* Till'd.
Delightful scientifick Shade!
For Knowledge, as for Pleasure made.
'Twas Gen'rous *DANBY* first enclos'd
The Waste, and in Parterres dispos'd;
Transform'd the Fashion of the Ground,
And Fenc'd it with a Rocky Mound;
The Figure disproportion'd chang'd,
Trees, Shrubs, and Plants in Order rang'd;
Stock'd it, with such excessive Store,
Only the spacious Earth has more:
At His Command the Plat was chose,
And *Eden* from the *Chaos* rose:
Confusion in a Moment fled,
And Roses blush'd where Thistles bred.
The *Portico* next, High he rear'd,
By Builders now so much rever'd;
(Which like some Rustick Beauty shows,
Who all her Charms to Nature owes;
Yet fires the Heart, and warms the Head,
No less than those in Cities bred;
Our Wonder equally does raise
With them, as well deserves our Praise.)
The Work of *Jones*'s Master-Hand:
Jones, the *Vitruvius* of our Land;
He drew the Plan, the Fabrick fixd,
With equal Strength, and Beauty mix'd:

With perfect Symmetry design'd;
Consummate, like the Donor's Mind . . .
There, where old *Cherwell* gently leads
His humid Train, along the Meads;
And courts fair *Isis*, but in vain,
Who laughs at all his am'rous Pain;
Away the scornful *Naid* turns,
For younger *Tamus*, *Isis* burns . . .
There 'tis we see Thee, *BOBART*, tend
Thy fav'rite Greens; from Harms defend
Exotick Plants, which finely Bred
In softer Soils, Thy Succour need;
Whose Birth far distant Countries claim,
Sent here in Honour to Thy Name.
To Thee the Strangers trembling fly,
For Shelter from our barb'rous Sky,
And murd'ring Winds, that frequent blow,
With cruel Drifts of Rain or Snow;
And dreadful Ills, both Fall and Spring,
On alien Vegetables bring.
Nor art thou less inclin'd to save,
Than they Thy gen'rous Aid to crave:
But with like Pleasure and Respect,
Thy darling Tribe Thou doest Protect: . . .
The rest, who will no Culture know,
But ceaseless Curse our Rains and Snow . . .

Thy *Hortus Siccus*[1] still receives:
In Tomes twice Ten, that Work immense!
By Thee compil'd at vast Expence;
With utmost Diligence amass'd,
And shall as many Ages last . . .

1. A *Hortus Siccus* is a collection of *Plants*, pasted upon
Paper, and kept Dry in a Book.

JOSEPH TRAPP
(1679–1747)

WILLIAM BROWNE
(1692–1774)

Born at Cherrington in Gloucestershire, Trapp studied at Wadham and was made a Fellow in 1704. He was the first Professor of Poetry in Oxford, from 1708 to 1718. He later (1721) became vicar of Christ Church in Newgate Street and (1733) rector of Harlington in Middlesex. Trapp's publications included the tragedy *Abra-mule, or Love and Empire* (1704) which was often reprinted; a translation of Virgil (1718–31) which was not well received; *Thoughts upon the Four Last Things: Death, Heaven, Judgment, Hell* (1734–35); miscellaneous sermons, and a translation of Milton, *Paradisus Amissus Latine Redditus* (1741–42). This epigram was written on the occasion of George I having bought the valuable library of John Moore, Bishop of Ely, and donated it to the University of Cambridge. Trapp's lines produced an impromptu rejoinder from the physician Sir William Browne, a graduate of Cambridge.

(i) On a Regiment being sent to Oxford, and a Present of Books to Cambridge, by George I., in 1715

The king, observing with judicious eyes,
The state of both his universities,
To Oxford sent a troop of horse; and why?
That learned body wanted loyalty.
To Cambridge books he sent, as well discerning
How much that loyal body wanted learning.

(ii)

The king to Oxford sent a troop of horse,
For Tories own no argument but force;
With equal skill to Cambridge books he sent,
For Whigs admit no force but argument.

GEORGE WOODWARD

(fl.1727–1730)

As well as *Poems on Several Occasions* of 1730, from which 'The Oxford Beauties' is taken, Woodward appears to have published a *Poem to the Glorious Memory of His Sacred Majesty, King George I* in 1727. A poem published in 1717, *Merton Walks: or the Oxford Beauties* has sometimes been attributed to him, but is more probably the work of John Dry. The poems by Dry and Woodward effectively form, with Amhurst's *Strephon's Revenge*, a small sub-genre of Oxford poems. (For a modern poem on 'the Oxford Beauties', see 'Women at Oxford' by Gwyn Williams, in *Foundation Stock*, 1974.) The Woodward of the 1730 volume was perhaps the George Woodward of Yealmpton in Devon, who matriculated at Wadham in 1718, aged fourteen.

The Oxford Beauties

Ye gentle Nymphs! that haunt fair *Isis* Streams,
Aid me in Visions and repeated Dreams;
By Beauty warm'd I touch the trembling String,
What Muse for Beauty will refuse to sing?
Ye *Oxford Belles*! my ravish'd Soul inspire
With all the Poet's and the Lover's Fire:
Beam on my Mind, excite the soft Alarm,
And make me conscious of each heav'nly Charm.
Lo! to my View a thousand Beauties rise,
In silent Rapture stand my wondring Eyes:
A modest Ardour dawns upon my Soul,
And vast Ideas in my Bosom roul.
Fain with their Merits would I grace my Lays,
And make my Verse immortal, as their Praise:
Oh! had I *Dorset*'s sweet, prevailing Art,
To speak the gentle Transports of my Heart!
Could I, like Him, awake the warbling Lyre,
And at each Motion kindle warm Desire.
Could I, like Him, the ev'ry Sense improve,
And make my Numbers equal to my Love!
Each am'rous Line should melt in soft Alarms,
And whisp'ring tell, from whom it stole it's Charms.

Sweet is *Sibilla*, fresh as Infant Day,
Bright without Pride, and Innocently gay:
Whene'er she wanders thro' the vernal Woods,
Or seeks the Murmurs of the falling Floods;
The vernal Woods seem ravish'd at the Sight,
And softer Murmurs speak the Floods Delight:
The *Sylvan Syrens* tune their choicest Strains,
And native Musick fills the list'ning Plains.
A Thousand *Cupids* wait upon the Fair,
Sport on her Breast, or revel in her Hair.

Shervina's Shape, her bright, unsully'd Charms,
Might set two warring Nations up in Arms:
See! with what Grace the soft Enchantress walks!
With what perswasive Eloquence She talks!

Such, or less fair, in antient Times was seen
On *Ida*'s shady Mount, the *Cyprian Queen*.
Sure! bounteous Heav'n, mistaking theirs for Thine,
Cast Thee, *Shervina*! in a Mould Divine.

Bright is *Dorella*, as the Morning Dawn,
Sweet as the Dews, that deck the open Lawn:
Soft as the Damask of the silken Rose,
Mild as when *Zephirus* on *Flora* blows.
Whene'er she speaks, Gods! how her heav'nly Tongue
Melts down the Passions of the list'ning Throng!
Like *Sampson*'s *Riddle*, she unfolds her Mind,
Where *Strength* and *Sweetness* both in One are joyn'd.

Fair *Anna*'s Charms allure the am'rous Youth
To taste the Joys of Innocence and Truth:
She's harmless as the Turtle of the Woods,
Sweet as the Vi'lets by the silver Floods.
No practis'd Smiles, or soft, affected Air
Sets off with cheating Grace the lovely Fair;
In native Beauty modestly she walks,
And charms alike, whene'er she looks or talks.

Eliza's Charms the heedless Boy surprize,
Whilst Youth and Beauty sparkle in her Eyes:
Endow'd with all, that can adorn the Fair,
A winning Accent, and a graceful Air.
Whene'er her Lyre begins some warbled Air,
Sweet are the Notes, as Nature made her Fair:
With sudden Arts she traps the roving Heart,
And shoots her pleasing Pains thro' every Part.

Andira's Beauties, like keen Light'ning, wound,
Her Words and Looks both equally confound: .
How gently-soft her lovely Ringlets flow,
Sport with the Gales, and fan the Neck below!
Her panting Breasts, like dying Turtles move,
Heave up and down, and wanton court to Love.
But when the sweet-deluding Syren sings,
Loves on her Lips rejoyce, and clap their silken Wings.

Soft *Margaretta* warms the panting Heart,
And shoots her Venom quick thro' ev'ry Part:
But when she smoothly swims the mazy Dance,
Now a Retreat, and then a bold Advance;
Heav'ns! how the Soul in Transport melts away,
Unable to withstand so bright a Day.

But oh! *Marinda*! how shall I rehearse
Thy matchless Charms in my too humble Verse?
Had not your Beauty Darts enough to wound,
But must we fall too by Poetick Sound?
Smooth flow your Numbers, as the gentle Stream,
Whilst *Woods* and *Turtles* are your softest Theme:
Your *modest Air* and *Manners* strong prevail,
In *which* your *Sappho*'s only said to fail;
Tho' free, yet chaste; tho' handsome, yet not vain;
Wise, without Pride; without Decieving, Plain.

Oh! let those Breasts be my Poetick Hill,
Those balmy Lips my *Heliconian* Rill:
Here let the Poet live the Heav'nly Day,
For ever on that Bosom let me lay,
And sing a whole Eternity away.

THOMAS TICKELL

(1685–1740)

Tickell was born near Bridekirk in Cumberland. In April 1701 he entered Queen's College, and was elected a Fellow in 1710. He did not, however, take orders. In 1726 he resigned his fellowship on marrying. He profited much from the patronage of Addison (whose works Tickell later edited) and, partly due to his influence, held a number of positions in the administration of Ireland. In 1715 he published a translation of Book I of the *Iliad*. This has sometimes been suspected (not least by Pope) to be the work of Addison. Always competent, Tickell's verse is rarely very individual. His elegy on Addison is perhaps his finest poem; Dr Johnson's judgement was that no 'more sublime or more elegant funeral-poem [was] to be found in the whole compass of English literature'.

from *Oxford: A Poem*

Me Fortune and kind Heaven's indulgent care
To famous Oxford and the Muses bear,
Where, of all ranks, the blooming youths combine
To pay due homage to the mighty Nine,
And snatch, with smiling joy, the laurel crown,
Due to the learned honours of the gown.
Here I, the meanest of the tuneful throng
Delude the time with an unhallow'd song,
Which thus my thanks to much-lov'd Oxford pays,
In no ungrateful, though unartful lays.

Where shall I first the beauteous scene disclose,
And all the gay variety expose?
For wheresoe'er I turn my wondering eyes,
Aspiring towers and verdant groves arise,
Immortal greens the smiling plains array,
And mazy rivers murmur all the way. . .
In equal state our rising structures shine,
Fram'd by such rules, and form'd by such design,
That here, at once surpriz'd and pleas'd, we view
Old Athens lost and conquer'd in the new;
More sweet our shades, more fit our bright abodes
For warbling Muses and inspiring Gods. . .

See, where the sacred Sheldon's haughty dome
Rivals the stately pomp of ancient Rome,
Whose form, so great and noble, seems design'd
T' express the grandeur of its founder's mind...

Next let the Muse record our Bodley's seat,
Nor aim at numbers, like the subject, great:
All hail, thou fabric, sacred to the Nine,
Thy fame immortal, and thy form divine!
Who to thy praise attempts the dangerous flight,
Should in thy various tongues be taught to write;
His verse, like thee, a lofty dress should wear,
And breathe the genius which inhabits there;
Thy proper lays alone can make thee live,
And pay that fame, which first thyself didst give.
So fountains, which through secret channels flow,
And pour above the floods they take below,
Back to their father Ocean urge their way,
And to the sea, the streams it gave, repay.

No more we fear the military rage,
Nurs'd up in some obscure barbarian age;
Nor dread the ruin of our arts divine,
From thick-skull'd heroes of the Gothic line,
Though pale the Romans saw those arms advance,
And wept their learning lost in ignorance.
Let brutal rage around its terrours spread,
The living murder, and consume the dead,
In impious fires let noblest writings burn,
And with their authors share a common urn;
Only, ye Fates, our lov'd Bodleian spare,
Be IT, and Learning's self shall be your care,
Here every art and every grace shall join,
Collected Phoebus here alone shall shine,
Each other seat be dark, and this be all divine...

With wonders fraught the bright Museum see,
Itself the greatest curiosity!
Where Nature's choicest treasure, all combin'd,
Delight at once, and quite confound the mind;

Ten thousand splendours strike the dazzled eye,
And form on Earth another galaxy.

Here colleges in sweet confusion rise,
There temples seem to reach their native skies;
Spires, towers, and groves, compose the various shew,
And mingled prospects charm the doubting view;
Who can deny their characters divine,
Without resplendent, and inspir'd within? . . .

Behold around, and see the living green
In native colours paints a blooming scene;
Th' eternal buds no deadly Winter fear,
But scorn the coldest season of the year;
Apollo sure will bless the happy place,
Which his own Daphne condescends to grace;
For here the everlasting laurels grow,
In every grotto, and on every brow. . .

See how the matchless youth their hours improve,
And in the glorious way to knowledge move!
Eager for fame, prevent the rising Sun,
And watch the midnight labours of the Moon.
Not tender years their bold attempts restrain,
Who leave dull Time, and hasten into man,
Pure to the soul, and pleasing to the eyes,
Like angels youthful, and like angels wise.

Some learn the mighty deeds of ages gone,
And, by the lives of heroes, form their own;
Now view the Granique choak'd with heaps of slain,
And warring worlds on the Pharsalian plain;
Now hear the trumpets clangour from afar,
And all the dreadful harmony of war;
Now trace those secret tricks that lost a state,
And search the fine-spun arts that made it great,
Correct those errours that its ruin bred,
And bid some long-lost empire rear its ancient head,

Others, to whom persuasive arts belong,
(Words in their looks, and music on their tongue)
Instructed by the wit of Greece and Rome,
Learn richly to adorn their native home;
Whilst listening crowds confess the sweet surprize,
With pleasure in their breasts, and wonder in their eyes.

Here curious minds the latent seeds disclose,
And Nature's darkest labyrinths expose;
Whilst greater souls the distant worlds descry,
Pierce to the out-stretch'd borders of the sky,
Enlarge the searching mind, and broad expand the
    eye. . .
Oxford, the goddess Muse's native home,
Inspir'd like Athens, and adorn'd like Rome!
Hadst thou of old been Learning's fam'd retreat,
And pagan Muses chose thy lovely seat,
O, how unbounded had their fiction been!
What fancy'd visions had adorn'd the scene!
Upon each hill a sylvan Pan had stood,
And every thicket boasted of a god;
Satyrs had frisk'd in each poetic grove,
And not a sream without its nymphs could move;
Each summit had the train of Muses show'd,
And Hippocrene in every fountain flow'd;
The tales, adorn'd with each poetic grace,
Had look'd almost as charming as the place. . .

O pleasing shades! O ever-green retreats!
Ye learned grottoes! and ye sacred seats!
Never may you politer arts refuse,
But entertain in peace the bashful Muse!
So may you be kind Heaven's distinguish'd care,
And may your fame be lasting, as 'tis fair!
Let greater Bards on fam'd Parnassus dream,
Or taste th' inspir'd Heliconian stream;
Yet, whilst our Oxford is the bless'd abode
Of every Muse, and every tuneful god,
Parnassus owns its honours far outdone,
And Isis boasts more Bards than Helicon.

NICHOLAS AMHURST
(1697?–1742)

Amhurst was expelled from St John's College, Oxford, for libertinism; he began publication (as 'Caleb D'Anvers') of *The Craftsman*, a paper dedicated to attacking Robert Walpole, which was first circulated in December 1726 and ran for some years, often selling a great many copies. Contributors included Bolingbroke (including his 'Remarks upon the History of England' and 'Dissertation upon Parties') and William Pulteney, the future Earl of Bath. Amhurst attacked his old University in several publications, such as his *Oculus Britanniæ: an Heroi-panegyrical poem on the University of Oxford* (1724) and *Terræ-Filius: or the secret history of the University of Oxford* (1726).

On the Images of the Nine Leaden Muses upon the new Printing-house in Oxford. An epigram

In *Oxford* Crouds of stupid Bards are found,
Where of all Places bright ones should abound;
Dull plodding Blockheads, without Sense or Fire,
Toil hard for Fame, and to the Bays aspire:
From deep Logicians shallow Wits commence,
Old Dogs at Rhime, no matter for the Sense;
If the Lines flow but smooth, and jingle well,
The Man's a Poet, and his Verses sell;
Nor is it strange, but rightly weigh the thing,
That our soft Bards so indolently sing,
Or that the Genius of the Place is dead,
When our inspiring Muses breathe in *Lead*:
High on the stately Dome, with Harp in hand,
Their lumpish Deities exalted stand,
Fix'd as a publick Mark, that all might know,
What wretched heavy Stuff they print below.

from *Strephon's Revenge: A Satire on the Oxford Toasts*

At length with Vengeance bursts my raging Vein,
Nor longer will th' imprison'd Wrath contain;
Thy Shame, oh! *Oxford*, in reluctant Verse,
Justice and Honour force me to rehearse:
Long did I strive inchain'd my Rage to keep,
And sooth'd the Tumults of my Blood asleep;
I wav'd th'ill-natur'd Task from time to time,
While filial Duty seem'd to check the Rhime,
But all in vain to quench my Gall conspire,
Rage spurs me on, a Fury strings my Lyre.

And see! to banish all remaining Fears,
Our Learned Mother to my Eyes appears;
'Twas Noon of Night, when blest with sweet Repose,
The pleasing Vision to my Fancy rose;
Thro' ambient Darkness, venerably bright,
The graceful Dame descended to my Sight;
A Lawrel-Crown her hoary Temples grac'd,
Her stately Limbs a sable Stole embrac'd;
Two River-Deities on either Side
Pour'd from their fruitful Urns the rushing Tide;
Isis and Charwell, thro' the World renown'd,
Their Brows with ample Wreaths of Sedges crown'd;
The Virgin-Muses gently march'd before,
And in their Hands immortal Cato bore;
Behind, the Arts and Sciences were seen,
With studious down-cast Looks and thoughtful Mein;
Ready to speak the rev'rend Form appear'd,
And list'ning, these propitious Words I heard.

"Fear not, my Son, in this degenerate Age
"To give a Loose to thy severest Rage,
"The stench of Brothels, and the filth of Stews,
"Call loud for Censure, and demand the Muse;
"Within our Walls a num'rous shameless Race
"(To useful Arts and Learning a Disgrace)

"Seduce to Folly the unpractis'd Youth,
"And turn his Footsteps from the Paths of Truth;
"While in our Schools declining Science fails,
"And Love alone and Gallantry prevails;
"Oxford seems tott'ring to her sudden Doom,
"And Athens a mere Paphos is become.

"Oh! rise in all thy Rage, chastise the Times,
"And Female Frauds unveil in daring Rhimes;
"Describe to view their Follies and Delights,
"Their viscious open Days, and hidden Nights;
"Nor think that Duty binds thee to conceal,
"What Justice, Truth and Virtue would reveal;
"To punish reigning Vice deserves our Love,
"And to be silent now, is to approve."
She said, and vanish'd from my gazing Sight,
Loos'd were my Eyes, and I awoke to Light.

Far hence let ev'ry softer Thought remove
Of childish Pity, and unmanly Love;
Let dull Compassion in my Bowels sleep,
And thro' my breast Satyric Whirlwinds sweep;
Ye Fiends and Furies my Revenge inspire.
Swell up my Heart and set my Soul on Fire;
Transfuse your rankest Gall into my Veins,
And keen as Oldham's, prompt my vengeful Strains.

My Prayer is heard; for now the rising Spleen
Swells all my Breast, and in my Face is seen;
With livid Flames my glaring Eye-balls roll,
And tenfold Vengeance wraps my lab'ring Soul:
My ev'ry Limb with boundless Fury shakes,
And round my Temples hiss the twining Snakes:
Hush'd are a while ev'n Love's tempestuous Tides,
And the fierce Torrent of my Blood subsides;
A while ev'n beauteous Laura I despise,
And all the Softness of my Nature dies;
Within my Breast no wonted Passions move,
Heal'd are my Wounds, and I forget to Love.

With gen'rous Grief I mourn our Oxford's Fate,
Her fading Glories and declining State;
The Muses, banish'd by an Harlot-train,
In other Lands renew the tuneful Strain;
Homer and Virgil quit disgrac'd the Field,
And to the skilful Dancing-Master yield;
Our Colleges grow elegantly dull,
Our Schools are empty, and our Taverns full.
The gowned Youth dissolves in am'rous Dreams,
And Pedantry to him all Learning seems;
He wastes his Bloom in Vanity and Ease,
And his chief Studies are to Dress and Please.

From Place to Place the Dunghill-tribe I fly,
And strive, in vain, to shut them from my Eye;
If thro' the lonely, smiling Meads I stray,
And by the Charwell pace my thoughtful Way,
Loud Female Laughters reach my distant Ears,
Before my Eyes the tawdry Manteau glares;
I shun th' approaching Sight, to Madness wrought,
And lose in Air the scatter'd Train of Thought.

If to the Tavern social Mirth invites,
With constant Pain I spend the joyless Nights;
Scrawl'd on the Glass I read the hated Names,
While my swoln Breast with Indignation flames;
The whining Blockheads, each his Toast assign,
And pall, with nauseous Praise, the gen'rous Wine;
I fret, I rail, with angry Bile I fume,
And broken Pipes and Glasses strew the Room.

Sometimes I turn the golden Ancients o'er,
Or Locke, the second Stagyrite, explore;
From Argument to Argument I stray,
And follow close where Reason points the Way;
Sometimes I drink at the Pierian Spring,
And trembling wanton on a youthful Wing;
But still the wonted Scene my Thought employs,
Cloggs all my Studies and dilutes my Joys.

Ev'n Sleep to me denies the needful Rest,
Or sleeping, Fancy haunts my troubled Breast;
The Plague and Torment of the Day returns,
And with Revenge my Soul in Slumber burns.

Nay, if at Church I bend the suppliant Knee,
Nor then from their damn'd Presence am I free;
The loathsome Object ev'n pursues me there,
I burst with Fury in the midst of Prayer;
Just as in fervent Transports I expire,
And my Soul mounts on Wings of hallow'd Fire,
Some haughty, worthless Minion meets my Sight,
And checks Devotion in its middle Height;
With Scorn upon each maudlin Face I dwell,
And with a pious, silent Madness swell.
When the loud Organ to the Anthem plays,
And thro' the various Notes harmonious strays,
O! how demure the list'ning Harlots leer,
And drink the Musick in at either Ear;
How the Sluts languish with deceitful Pride,
And ogling drop the pretty Head aside:
In Church they practice each new Female Air,
And to a Playhouse turn the House of Prayer.

Well for the Church may pious Christians fear,
And from its Dangers judge its Downfal near,
Since it is now become the publick Mart,
Where female Quacks display their Emp'rick Art.
Hither for Sale throng many a shining Toast,
The lawful Goods of him that proffers most;
Beauties of every Sort and Size appear,
That please all Fancies and all Prices bear
The Tall and Short, the Jolly and the Lean,
Of every Age from Forty to Fifteen;
Black, Brown and Fair are rang'd in different Pews,
That amorous Customers may pick and chuse:
Here sanguine Youths, dispos'd for married Lives,
And future Parsons are supply'd with Wives . . .

WILLIAM MASON

(1725–1797)

Mason, whose father was vicar of Holy Trinity in Kingston-upon-Hull, entered St John's College, Cambridge in 1742. He took his BA in 1745 and—largely through the friendly influence of Thomas Gray—was nominated for a fellowship at Pembroke College to which, after some difficulties, he was elected in 1749. His elegy for Pope, *Musæus*, was published in 1747 and proved very popular. In the following year, 1748, he published his *Isis: A Monologue*, a response to some Oxford scandals of the time in which both drunkenness and support for the Jacobite cause played a part. Thomas Warton responded with *The Triumph of Isis* (see below). Mason later became vicar of Aston in south Yorkshire (1754) and a canon of York (1762). His other publications included two tragedies, *Elfrida* (1752) and *Caractacus* (1759), and his didactic poem *The English Garden* (1772–82). He was one of Gray's executors and his editing and publishing of *The Poems of Mr. Gray, with Memoirs Prefixed* (1755) was a more important contribution to English literature than any of his own original work.

from *Isis: A Monologue*

'. . . Ah, I remember well yon beechen spray,
There Addison first tuned his polished lay;
'Twas there great Cato's form first met his eye,
In all the pomp of freeborn majesty.
"My son (he cried), observe this mien with awe,
In solemn lines the strong resemblance draw;
The piercing notes shall strike each *British* ear;
Each British eye shall drop the patriot tear;
And, roused to glory by this nervous strain,
Each youth shall spurn at Slavery's abject reign,
Shall guard with Cato's zeal Britannia's laws,
And speak, and act, and bleed, in Freedom's cause."'
The Hero spoke, the Bard assenting bow'd,
The lay to liberty and Cato flow'd;
While Echo, as she roved the vale along,
Join'd the strong cadence of his Roman song.
'But ah! how stillness slept upon the ground,
How mute Attention check'd each rising sound;

Scarce stole a breeze to wave the lofty spray,
Scarce trill'd sweet Philomel her softest lay,
When Locke walk'd musing forth; e'en now I view
Majestic Wisdom throned upon his brow,
View Candour smile upon his modest cheek,
And from his eye all Judgment's radiance break.
'Twas here the sage his manly zeal express'd,
Here stripp'd vain Falsehood of her gaudy vest;
Here Truth's collected beams first fill'd his mind,
Ere long to burst in blessings on mankind;
Ere long to show to Reason's purged eye,
That "Nature's first best gift was liberty."
'Proud of this wondrous son, sublime I stood
(While louder surges swell'd my rapid flood);
Then vain as Niobe exulting cried,
Ilissus! roll thy famed Athenian tide;
Though Plato's steps oft mark'd thy neighbouring glade,
Though fair Lycœum lent its awful shade,
Though every academic green impress'd
Its image full on thy reflecting breast,
Yet my pure stream shall boast as proud a name,
And Britain's Isis flow with Attic fame.
'Alas! how changed! where now that Attic boast?
See! Gothic Licence rage o'er all my coast.
See! Hydra Faction spread its impious reign,
Poison each breast, and madden every brain.
Hence frontless crowds that, not content to fright
The blushing Cynthia from her throne of night,
Blast the fair face of day; and madly bold,
To Freedom's foes infernal orgies hold;
To Freedom's foes, ah! see the goblet crown'd!
Hear plausive shouts to Freedom's foes resound!
The horrid notes my refluent waters daunt,
The Echoes groan, the Dryads quit their haunt;
Learning, that once to all diffused her beam,
Now sheds by stealth a partial private gleam
In some lone cloister's melancholy shade.
Where a firm few support her sickly head;
Despised, insulted by the barbarous train,

Who scour, like Thracia's moon-struck rout, the plain,
Sworn foes like them to all the Muse approves,
All Phœbus favours, or Minerva loves . . .'

THOMAS WARTON
(1728–1790)

Born in Basingstoke, where his father was vicar (Thomas Warton the elder was Professor of Poetry at Oxford from 1718 to 1728), Warton was admitted a commoner of Trinity College, Oxford in 1743. He was made a Scholar soon afterwards. In 1747 he published *The Pleasures of Melancholy*, written when he was only seventeen; he was made a Fellow in 1751 and in 1757 became Professor of Poetry. He was rector of Kidlington and of Hill Farrance (in Somerset). He was an important pioneer of the study of early poetry—as in his *Observations on the Faerie Queene of Spenser* (1754), his edition of Milton's minor poems (1785), and, above all, in his remarkable *History of English Poetry* (1774–81). Warton's own poetry is generally bookish and derivative, but not without sparks of life. His fondness for pipe and tankard finds exuberant expression in his 'Panegyric on Oxford Ale'.

from *The Triumph Of Isis, Occasioned by Isis An Elegy*

Ye fretted pinnacles, ye fanes sublime,
Ye towers that wear the mossy vest of time;
Ye massy piles of old munificence,
At once the pride of learning and defence;
Ye cloisters pale, that lengthening to the sight,
To contemplation, step by step, invite;
Ye high-arch'd walks, where oft the whispers clear
Of harps unseen have swept the poet's ear;
Ye temples dim, where pious duty pays
Her holy hymns of ever-echoing praise;
Lo! your lov'd Isis, from the bordering vale,
With all a mother's fondness bids you hail!—
Hail, Oxford, hail! of all that's good and great,
Of all that's fair, the guardian and the seat;
Nurse of each brave pursuit, each generous aim,
By truth exalted to the throne of fame!
Like Greece in science and in liberty,
As Athens learn'd, as Lacedemon free!
Ev'n now, confess'd to my adoring eyes,
In awful ranks thy gifted sons arise.

Tuning to knightly tale his British reeds,
Thy genuine bards immortal Chaucer leads:
His hoary head o'erlooks the gazing quire,
And beams on all around celestial fire.
With graceful step see Addison advance,
The sweetest child of Attic elegance:
See Chillingworth the depths of Doubt explore,
And Selden ope the rolls of ancient lore:
To all but his belov'd embrace deny'd,
See Locke lead Reason, his majestic bride:
See Hammond pierce Religion's golden mine,
And spread the treasur'd stores of truth divine.

All who to Albion gave the arts of peace,
And best the labours plann'd of letter'd ease;
Who taught with truth, or with persuasion mov'd;
Who sooth'd with numbers, or with sense improv'd;
Who rang'd the powers of reason, or refin'd,
All that adorn'd or humaniz'd the mind;
Each priest of health, that mix'd the balmy bowl,
To rear frail man, and stay the fleeting soul;
All croud around, and echoing to the sky,
Hail, Oxford, hail! with filial transport cry.

And see yon sapient train! with liberal aim,
'Twas theirs new plans of liberty to frame;
And on the Gothic gloom of slavish sway
To shed the dawn of intellectual day.
With mild debate each musing feature glows,
And well-weigh'd counsels mark their meaning brows.
"Lo! these the leaders of thy patriot line,"
A Raleigh, Hampden, and a Somers shine.
These from thy source the bold contagion caught,
Their future sons the great example taught:
While in each youth th' hereditary flame
Still blazes, unextinguish'd and the same! ...

from *A Panegyric on Oxford Ale*

— Mea nec Falernæ
Temperant vites, neque Formiani
Pocula colles.

Horace

Balm of my cares, sweet solace of my toils,
Hail, JUICE benignant! O'er the costly cups
Of riot-stirring wine, unwholesome draught,
Let Pride's loose sons prolong the wasteful night;
My sober evening let the tankard bless,
With toast embrown'd, and fragrant nutmeg fraught,
While the rich draught with oft-repeated whiffs
Tobacco mild improves. Divine repast!
Where no crude surfeit, or intemperate joys
Of lawless Bacchus reign; but o'er my soul
A calm Lethean creeps; in drowsy trance
Each thought subsides, and sweet oblivion wraps
My peaceful brain, as if the leaden rod
Of magic Morpheus o'er mine eyes had shed
Its opiate influence. What tho' sore ills
Oppress, dire want of chill-dispelling coals
Or cheerful candle (save the make-weight's gleam
Haply remaining) heart-rejoicing ALE
Cheers the sad scene, and every want supplies.
    Meantime, not mindless of the daily task
Of Tutor sage, upon the learned leaves
Of deep SMIGLECIUS much I meditate;
While ALE inspires, and lends its kindred aid,
The thought-perplexing labour to pursue,
Sweet Helicon of Logic! But if friends
Congenial call me from the toilsome page,
To Pot-house I repair, the sacred haunt,
Where, ALE, thy votaries in full resort
Hold rites nocturnal. In capacious chair
Of monumental oak and antique mould,
That long has stood the rage of conquering years ...
Studious of ease, and provident, I place
My gladsome limbs ...

89

Hail, TICKING! surest guardian of distress!
Beneath thy shelter, pennyless I quaff
The cheerful cup, nor hear with hopeless heart
New oysters cry'd;—tho' much the Poet's friend,
Ne'er yet attempted in poetic strain,
Accept this tribute of poetic praise!
   Nor Proctor thrice with vocal heel alarms
Our joys secure, nor deigns the lowly roof
Of Pot-house snug to visit: wiser he
The splendid tavern haunts, or coffee-house
Of JAMES or JUGGINS, where the grateful breath
Of loath'd tobacco ne'er diffus'd its balm;
But the lewd spendthrift, falsely deem'd polite,
While steams around the fragrant Indian bowl,
Oft damns the vulgar sons of humbler ALE:
In vain—the Proctor's voice arrests their joys;
Just fate of wanton pride and loose excess!
   Nor less by day delightful is thy draught,
All-pow'rful ALE! whose sorrow-soothing sweets
Oft I repeat in vacant afternoon,
When tatter'd stockings ask my mending hand
Not unexperienc'd; while the tedious toil
Slides unregarded. Let the tender swain
Each morn regale on nerve-relaxing tea,
Companion meet of languor-loving nymph:
Be mine each morn with eager appetite
And hunger undissembled, to repair
To friendly buttery; there on smoking crust
And foaming ALE to banquet unrestrain'd,
Material breakfast! . . .
   With ALE irriguous, undismay'd I hear
The frequent dun ascend my lofty dome
Importunate: whether the plaintive voice
Of Laundress shrill awake my startled ear;
Or Barber spruce with supple look intrude;
Or Taylor with obsequious bow advance;
Or Groom invade me with defying front
And stern demeanour, whose emaciate steeds
(Whene'er or Phoebus shone with kindlier beams,
Or luckier chance the borrow'd boots supply'd)

Had panted oft beneath my goring steel.
In vain they plead or threat: all-pow'rful ALE
Excuses new supplies, and each descends
With joyless pace, and debt-despairing looks:
E'en SPACEY with indignant brow retires,
Fiercest of duns! and conquer'd quits the field . . .

Verses on Sir Joshua Reynolds's Painted Window at New College, Oxford

Ah, stay thy treacherous hand, forbear to trace
Those faultless forms of elegance and grace!
Ah, cease to spread the bright transparent mass,
With Titian's pencil, o'er the speaking glass!
Nor steal, by strokes of art with truth combin'd,
The fond illusions of my wayward mind!
For long, enamour'd of a barbarous age,
A faithless truant to the classic page;
Long have I lov'd to catch the simple chime
Of minstrel-harps, and spell the fabling rime;
To view the festive rites, the knightly play,
That deck'd heroic Albion's elder day;
To mark the mouldering halls of barons bold,
And the rough castle, cast in giant mould;
With Gothic manners Gothic arts explore,
And muse on the magnificence of yore.

But chief, enraptur'd have I lov'd to roam,
A lingering votary, the vaulted dome,
Where the tall shafts, that mount in massy pride,
Their mingling branches shoot from side to side;
Where elfin sculptors, with fantastic clew,
O'er the long roof their wild embroidery drew;
Where SUPERSTITION with capricious hand
In many a maze the wreathed window plann'd,
With hues romantic ting'd the gorgeous pane,
To fill with holy light the wondrous fane;
To aid the builder's model, richly rude,
By no Vitruvian symmetry subdu'd;
To suit the genius of the mystic pile:

Whilst as around the far-retiring ile,
And fretted shrines, with hoary trophies hung,
Her dark illumination wide she flung,
With new solemnity, the nooks profound,
The caves of death, and the dim arches frown'd.
From bliss long felt unwillingly we part:
Ah, spare the weakness of a lover's heart!
Chase not the phantoms of my fairy dream,
Phantoms that shrink at Reason's painful gleam!
That softer touch, insidious artist, stay,
Nor to new joys my struggling breast betray!

Such was a pensive bard's mistaken strain.—
But, oh, of ravish'd pleasures why complain?
No more the matchless skill I call unkind,
That strives to disenchant my cheated mind.
For when again I view thy chaste design,
The just proportion, and the genuine line;
Those native portraitures of Attic art,
That from the lucid surface seem to start;
Those tints, that steal no glories from the day,
Nor ask the sun to lend his streaming ray:
The doubtful radiance of contending dies,
That faintly mingle, yet distinctly rise;
'Twixt light and shade the transitory strife;
The feature blooming with immortal life:
The stole in casual foldings taught to flow,
Not with ambitious ornaments to glow;
The tread majestic, and the beaming eye,
That lifted speaks its commerce with the sky;
Heaven's golden emanation, gleaming mild
O'er the mean cradle of the Virgin's child:
Sudden, the sombrous imagery is fled,
Which late my visionary rapture fed:
Thy powerful hand has broke the Gothic chain,
And brought my bosom back to truth again;
To truth, by no peculiar taste confin'd,
Whose universal pattern strikes mankind;
To truth, whose bold and unresisted aim
Checks frail caprice, and fashion's fickle claim;

To truth, whose charms deception's magic quell,
And bind coy Fancy in a stronger spell.
Ye brawny Prophets, that in robes so rich,
At distance due, possess the crisped nich;
Ye rows of Patriarchs, that sublimely rear'd
Diffuse a proud primeval length of beard:
Ye Saints, who, clad in crimson's bright array,
More pride than humble poverty display:
Ye Virgins meek, that wear the palmy crown
Of patient faith, and yet so fiercely frown:
Ye Angels, that from clouds of gold recline,
But boast no semblance to a race divine:
Ye tragic Tales of legendary lore,
That draw devotion's ready tear no more;
Ye Martyrdoms of unenlighten'd days,
Ye Miracles, that now no wonder raise:
Shapes, that with one broad glare the gazer strike,
Kings, Bishops, Nuns, Apostles, all alike!
Ye Colours, that th' unwary sight amaze,
And only dazzle in the noontide blaze!
No more the sacred window's round disgrace,
But yield to Grecian groupes the shining space.
Lo, from the canvas Beauty shifts her throne,
Lo, Picture's powers a new formation own!
Behold, she prints upon the crystal plain,
With her own energy, th' expressive stain!
The mighty Master spreads his mimic toil
More wide, nor only blends the breathing oil;
But calls the lineaments of life compleat
From genial alchymy's creative heat;
Obedient forms to the bright fusion gives,
While in the warm enamel Nature lives.

   REYNOLDS, 'tis thine, from the broad window's
         height,
To add new lustre to religious light:
Not of its pomp to strip this ancient shrine,
But bid that pomp with purer radiance shine:
With arts unknown before, to reconcile
The willing Graces to the Gothic pile.

93

ANONYMOUS

(1767)

The Prologue to The Oxonian in Town, *played at Covent Garden, 1767*

Fresh from the Schools, behold an Oxford smart,
No dupe to science, no dull slave of art;
As to our dress, faith, Ladies! to say truth,
It is a little awkward and uncouth;
No sword, cockade, to lure you to our arms—
But then this airy tassel hath its charms.
What mortal Oxford laundress can withstand
This, and the graces of a well-starched band?
In this array, our spark, with winning air,
Boldly accosts the froth-compelling fair;
Fast by the tub, with folded arms he stands
And sees his surplice whiten in her hands,
And as she dives into the soapy floods,
Wishes almost—himself were in the suds.
  Sometimes the car he drives impetuous on.
Cut, lash and flash, a very Phaethon,
Swift as the fiery coursers of the sun
Up hill and down, his raw-boned hackneys run,
Leaving, with heat half-dead, and dust half-blind,
Turnpikes and bawling hosts unpaid behind.
  You think, perhaps, we read—perhaps we may—
The news, a pamphlet, or the last new play;
But for the scribblers of the Augustan Age,
Horace and such queer mortals—not a page;
His brilliant sterling wit we justly hold
More brilliant far, transformed to sterling gold.
Though Euclid we digest without much pain
And solve his problems into brisk champaign.
Fired with this juice—why let the Proctor come,
"Young men, 'tis late—'tis time you were at home."
"Zounds! are you here," we cry, "with your dull rules,
Like Banquo's ghost, to push us from our stools."
  Such are the studies smarts pursue at college,
Oh, we are great proficients in such knowledge.

SAMUEL BISHOP

(1731–1795)

Educated at Merchant Taylors' School, Bishop became a Scholar of St John's College, Oxford, in 1750. He later became headmaster of his old school and rector of St Martin Outwich in London. He was an assured and facile composer of social verse.

Epigram CCXXIII

By the statutes, pro forma, in Oxford, 'tis said,
Certain lectures for certain degrees, must be read:
Which, because there's no audience, except the bare
    walls,
Wall-Lectures, each candidate properly calls.
For Oxford, I feel, what we all feel beside;
I think on't with pleasure; I name it with pride;
But this statute, methinks, must defective appear:—
That which binds some to read—should have bound
    some to hear!

CHARLES BATHURST

(fl.1775)

British Library Add. MS. 61910 is a collection headed 'Charles Bathurst Verses'. His work, which seems never to have been published, is pleasantly accomplished in a pre-Romantic idiom. It includes an elegy 'On the Death of Mr. Gray' (i.e. Thomas Gray) and a 'Sonnet Written in Gray's Poems' (1777), a poem 'To a Lady on returning Rousseau's Nouvelle Eloise which she had lent to the author' (dated 1776) and translations from Dante, Petrarch, Preti, and Quevedo, as well as original poems in Italian, Latin, and Greek.

Written In Christ Church Meadow Oxford, Aug. 1773

> Gently o'er thy sedgy bed,
>   Sleepy *Cherwell*, wind thy way—
> May no Heifer's wanton tread
>   Rudely tear thy bank away;
>
> May no boist'rous wind of Even
>   Dare disturb thy placid stream;
> Still reflect th'expanded Heav'n,
>   Still the Sun's yet-glimmering beam.
>
> I nor bid your drowsy flood
>   Briskly murmur through the meads;
> Such, as when in angry mood
>   Winter choaks your way with weeds.
>
> I nor ask the lucid Stream
>   Bright Hygeia loves to pour;
> On whose bank the Poet's dream
>   Teems with Fancy's wildest store;
>
> Wrapt in calm, how like thine own,
>   Pleas'd thy current I survey,
> While not one leaf floating down,
>   Marks thy melancholy way.

Thus through Life's uncertain scene,
    Would I shape my constant course;
While my bosom's calm serene,
    Felt no Passion's boistrous force:

Thus unheeded & unknown,
    Calm contented would I stray;
While nor Fortune nor Renown,
    Mark'd the tenor of my way.

Still I'd take thee for my guide,
    End with thee as I begun;
And in Isis' purer tide,
    Lose each sully of my own.

THOMAS MAURICE

(1754–1824)

Educated at St John's College and University College, Oxford, Maurice took holy orders, and was vicar of Cudham, in Kent, from 1804. In 1799 he had been appointed assistant librarian in the British Museum. He published poems and tragedies and a series of works on India, notably his *Indian Antiquities* (1791–97), *The History of Hindostan* (1795–99), and *The Modern History of Hindostan* (1802–10).

from *The Oxonian*

> ... I issue forth
> To seek the mansion of a learned sage,
> Y'clep'd a Tutor; him aloof I ken,
> On elbows twain of antient chair reclin'd,
> With cobwebs hung, by time's sharp tooth defac'd,
> Midst volumes pil'd on volumes all around,
> And dusty manuscripts; treasures I ween
> Of antient lore: He sullen from his chair
> Reclines not, 'till with many an aukward bow
> And strain right humble I implore his grace.
> Questions the sage proposes, dark, perplex'd;
> Of various import—and to sound my skill
> O'er many an author turns, to me well known,
> Virgil or Horace, or the dreadful page
> Of Homer, name accurst—descending hence
> His steps at awful distance I pursue,
> Admiring much my strange unwonted garb,
> And wond'rous head-piece; till at length we reach
> The mansion of a venerable Seer,
> Second alone of all the letter'd race,
> Who opes a mighty volume, graced with rows
> Of various names, in seemly order rang'd;
> 'Midst these the humblest of the muse's train
> Enrolls his name: and Isis hails her son.
> Some mystic sounds pronounc's, with trembling lips
> The sacred page I kiss, and from his hand
> A book receive, of small regard to see,

With godly counsels fraught, and wholesome rules;
Which ill betide the wight who dares offend.
The wonted fees discharg'd, I haste away
To join the circle of my old compeers,
Sever'd by cruel fate—The hearty shake,
The friendly welcome, go alternate round:
And that blest day, 'till eve's remotest hour,
Is sacred to our joys—Its choicest stores
The genial larder opes; exhausted deep,
Even to its inmost hoards, the buttery groans.
But now the bottle rolls its ample round,
Kindling to rapture each congenial soul;
The burst of merriment, the joyous catch
Ring round the roofs incessant—much is talk'd
Of past exploits, and grievous tasks impos'd
By former tyrants; tyrants now no more.
Transported with the thought, in frantic joy
I raise my arm, and 'midst surrounding shouts,
Quaff the full bumper; ah *full* dearly rued!
Stern fortune, thus ev'n in the cup of bliss
To mix the dregs of woe—a deadly hue
Sudden invests my cheeks, my fainting soul
Is fill'd with horrid loathings and strange pangs,
Unfelt before, convulsing all my frame:
Med'cines are vain, or serve but to augment
My grievous plight, 'till some experienc'd friend
Lead me to neighb'ring couch, where grateful sleep
Soon o'er my senses sheds her opiate balm . . .

RICHARD POLWHELE

(1760–1835)

Born at Truro, and educated at the Grammar School there, Polwhele matriculated as a commoner at Christ Church in 1778 but left without taking a degree. He was ordained in 1782, and for the next twelve years held curacies near Exeter, mixing with literary society there. From 1794 he held a living at Helston in Cornwall. He died in the city of his birth. He was a poet and topographer, historian and memoirist. Some of his best work is to be found in his translation of *The Idylls, Epigrams, and Fragments of Theocritus, Bion, and Moschus, with the Elegies of Tyrtœus* (1786), which was often reprinted. His other voluminous productions include histories of both Devon and Cornwall, sermons, a Cornish-English vocabulary, *An essay on marriage, adultery and divorce* (1823), and some interesting *Traditions and Recollections* (1826).

from *The Follies of Oxford, &c.*

Well,—Since my HENRY bids me trace
The Manners of the *College-Race*;
Such as it is, my Verse shall chime
Or classic Lays, or Runic Rhyme!
To thee perhaps, these Lines may haste
Unpolish'd by the Hand of *Taste*:
Yet, while in rougher Traits, they rise
To hurt the *Critic's* purged Eyes,
With pleasure shall a *Friend* peruse
The *Sketches* of an OXFORD *Muse*.
And, not in vain, the *Muse* may try
To shoot the *Follies* as they fly!—
For here, the *motley Brood* display
Their Plumes, so boldly to the Day,—
That wing'd by no Finess of Art
Speeds thro' mid Air, the unerring Dart! . . .
By *Fashion* sway'd, few Gownsmen here
To *Conscience* lend a listening Ear!
When now, the frowning *Pedagogue*
No more can persecute, or flog.

The raw, unfetter'd *Boy* behold
With soaring Hopes of Freedom bold!
And yet the poor misguided Elf
(No Power of thinking for himself)
Gives to the *Statutes* (nothing loath)
The Prostitution of an Oath,
And pleas'd subscribes by *Custom* led
To Articles, he never read!
Just enter'd at the *College-Gate*
Seduction tempts him with a Bait—
And soon, of unsuspecting Heart,
He falls, the Victim of her Art!

From *Loungers* of a listless Day
Learning flies ridicul'd away!
Enough—if learnt the Logic Rules
For Disputations in the *Schools*!
See Crowds, high-vested with *Degrees*
Just qualified—to pay the Fees!
As well might ALMA for a Purse,
With D. D. dignify a Horse! . . .

Yet must *each Student* try his Fate in
The Wisdom of the Greek and Latin?
And, indiscriminately class'd,
Does HOMER suit the various Taste?
Is every Student doom'd to read
PLATO's, or ARISTOTLE's Creed?
All, with a View to bless Mankind,
Behold for different Fates design'd!
While *that* asserts his *Country's Laws*
This vindicates the *Christian Cause*;
A Third exerts the healing Trade,
While *this* must preach, and *that* must plead:
Yet, with no Lessons to prepare
Or for the *Pulpit*, or the *Bar*,
Here all must tread the same dull Round
To gather *Weeds* on *Classic Ground*;
Alas!—regardless of the Toils
That wait them in more steril Soils! . . .

101

Ye FELLOWS, who demurely doze
Blest with Stupidity's Repose,
(And sure, unless the Poet lies
"'Tis arrant Folly to be wise")
Say, should the MUSE hold forth to view
Your Pictures, drawn severely true—
Say would not *Shame* in Blushes rise,
Oft' as the Colours caught your Eyes?
Ah no—so bronzed o'er with Brass
Shame never ting'd a *Fellow*'s Face;—
What then avails thy Muse so long
To waste, in whipping *Posts*, a Thong.
What though thou lash the Fools, behold
Still in the Paths of *Folly* bold,
With all the Glare of Impudence
They rove, secure from *Shame*, or *Sense*:
Still, listless, in the *Common Room*,
They dream of Happiness to come,
And, weary of their learned Life,
Sigh for a *Living*, or a *Wife*! . . .

Lo where St. MARY's antique Tower
Proud rising crowns the *Classic Bower*,
A motley mercenary Herd
Ordain'd to propagate the Word,
These with *peculiar* Grace impart
Religious Comfort to the Heart!
Oft' while their Powers might raise a Sneer,
Or draw from PITY's Eye the Tear,
MORPHEUS lets fall his gentle dews
And Slumbers creep along the Pews!
Go shameless Tribe, and walk the Town,
Vile Hirelings in your draggled Gown;
Or, seiz'd with a religious Qualm,
At MERTON sing the hundredth Psalm,
With *Scouts* the Chorus join, or hail
Their WARDEN with—a Pot of Ale!
The Liturgy for Half-pence read,
Or bury for a Groat a Head;
While (Congregation, staring round)
Ye reel o'er consecrated Ground,
And, thus prepar'd your Souls to save,
Totter into the yawning Grave! . . .

WILLIAM LISLE BOWLES

(1762–1850)

Born at King's Sutton in Northamptonshire, Bowles was educated at Winchester and Trinity College, Oxford. In 1804 he became rector of Bremhill in Wiltshire, and later (1828) became a Canon Residentiary of Salisbury. His first publication was *Fourteen Sonnets* (Bath, 1789); by 1805 this had reached (with additions) a ninth edition. The young Coleridge declared (surely a little extravagantly) that Bowles's sonnets had done his 'heart more good than all the other books he ever read excepting the Bible'. Certainly the graceful sentimentality of Bowles's sonnets was well fitted to appeal to the new Romantic sensibility. Bowles's longer poems, which include *The Spirit of Discovery* (1805) and *St. John in Patmos* (1833), contain some pleasant, if unspectacular, meditative and descriptive verse. High Church in disposition, Bowles also published antiquarian works, sermons, and a number of pamphlets on such topics as Church politics and the Poor Laws.

Oxford Revisited

I never hear the sound of thy glad bells,
   Oxford, and chime harmonious, but I say,
   Sighing to think how time has worn away,
Some spirit speaks in the sweet tone that swells,
   Heard after years of absence, from the vale
   Where Cherwell winds. Most true it speaks the tale
Of days departed, and its voice recalls
   Hours of delight and hope in the gay tide
   Of life, and many friends now scattered wide
By many fates. Peace be within thy walls!
I have scarce heart to visit thee; but yet,
   Denied the joys sought in thy shades,—denied
   Each better hope, since my poor Harriet died,
What I have owed to thee, my heart can ne'er forget!

At Oxford, 1786

Bereave me not of Fancy's shadowy dreams,
  Which won my heart, or when the gay career
  Of life begun, or when at times a tear
Sat sad on memory's cheek—though loftier themes
Await the awakened mind to the high prize
  Of wisdom, hardly earned with toil and pain,
  Aspiring patient; yet on life's wide plain
Left fatherless, where many a wanderer sighs
Hourly, and oft our road is lone and long,
  'Twere not a crime should we a while delay
  Amid the sunny field; and happier they
Who, as they journey, woo the charm of song,
To cheer their way;—till they forget to weep,
And the tired sense is hushed, and sinks to sleep.

HENRY HEADLEY

(1765–1788)

Born in Norfolk, Headley was an undergraduate at Trinity, admitted a commoner in 1782. Like his fellow student William Lisle Bowles, Headley was much influenced by Thomas Warton, then a Fellow of Trinity. Headley's *Select Beauties of Ancient English Poetry* (1787) was important in the revival of interest in Elizabethan poetry; he contributed essays to the *Gentleman's Magazine* on, among others, Milton, Drayton, Crashaw, and Quarles. Most of his own poetry is melancholic and plaintive, but the verses printed here show that he also possessed a sense of humour. Always of fragile health, he died of consumption after a disappointed romance and a misjudged marriage. In his 'Monody on Henry Headley', Bowles remembered his friend:

> To every gentle Muse in vain allied,
> In youth's full early morning Headley died!
> Too long had sickness left her pining trace,
> With slow, still touch, on each decaying grace:
> Untimely sorrow marked his thoughtful mien!
> Despair upon his languid smile was seen! . . .
>
> Nor ceased he yet to stray, where, winding wild,
> The Muse's path his drooping steps beguiled,
> Intent to rescue some neglected rhyme,
> Lone-blooming, from the mournful waste of time.

A Parody on Gray's Elegy, Written in a Country Church yard, the Author leaving College

Et dulces moriens reminiscitur Argos.

Virg.

The sullen Tom proclaims the parting day
In bullying tone congenial to his place,
The Christ Church misses homeward trip to pray
And High-street leave to solitude and space;
O'er the dim scene in stillness steals the night,
Save where the whistling 'prentice bars the shutter,
Or rapid mail-coach wheels its droning flight,
Or tinkling plates forebode th' approach of supper;

Save near yon tower, where now she sits and sighs,
Curses some miscreant Raph that Luckless Lass,
And as his sixpence by the Moon she tries
Shakes her despairing head and finds it brass.

Beneath those domes in Gothic grandeur grey
Where rears that spire its old fantastic crest,
Snug in their mouldy cells from day to day
Like bottled wasps the Sons of Science rest;

Th' unwelcome call of business-bringing morn,
The dull ox lowing from his neighbouring shed,
The tythe pig's clarion, or sow gelder's horn,
Ne'er 'wake these fatt'ning sleepers from their bed;

Their bile no smoking chimneys e'er provoke,
No busy breeding dame disturbs their nap,
Their double chins no squalling bantlings stroke,
Climbing their knees for rattles, or for pap;

Let not pert Folly mock their lecture's toil,
Their annual Gaudy's joys, and meetings mellow,
Nor Quin's ghost hear with a disdainful smile,
The short and simple commons of a Fellow;

The boast of cooks, the lordly venison,
The rich ragou, and liver-tickling jelly,
Down the red lane inevitably run
And at the best can only fill the belly.

Nor you, ye spinsters, these poor men abuse,
(Tis want of money rather than of wit)
If thus their backward threepence they refuse,
To your inviting charms and Billy Pitt;[1]

Can Madan's voice provoke the dull cold clay,
Or Price's system that implies a wife,[2]
Or aught the rosy goddess has to say,
When once a man is bent on single life?

Perhaps mid these unsocial yews is placed,
Some head once member of the "Chosen Few."[3]
Hands that the dazzling diamond might have graced,
Or tipt with extasy the billet-doux;

But Fashion to their eyes her motley page
Rich with the rags of France would ne'er unroll;
Through this they lost "The Ton," "the Thing," "the
    Rage,"
And all the soft enamel of the soul.

Full many a bawdy pun and joke obscene,
Penn'd as he pass'd by some unlucky dog,
On the lone ale-house window lurk unseen,
Or waste their waggish sweetness in a bog.

Some birth-day Colonel, with undaunted breast,
May here do generals, or defy the proctor,
Some lee-shore Admiral here at calm may rest,
And mutely read wall lectures for a doctor.

To rule each cackling circle coxcomb smitten,
To cheat their tradesmen and despise their betters,
To spell their titles in the Red-Book written,
(Should fate have kindly taught them but their letters.)

Their lot forbids—nor circumscribes alone
Their decent virtues, but their crimes, you'll find,
Forbids with fawning face to dog the throne,
And 'whelm with war and taxes half mankind,

The surly pangs of stubborn truth to hide,
To hush the tumults of rebellious shame,
To feast the pamper'd taste of glutton Pride
With sweet sauce piping hot from Learning's flame.

Far from the turbid paths of madd'ning strife
Their fire-side wishes never learn to stray,
Along the turnpike road of even life,
They keep the jog-trot tenour of their way;

Yet even their bones from surgeons to protect,
Some friendly tablet in the chapel aile,
With sniv'ling cherubs, and fat angels deck'd,
Excites the casual tribute of a smile,

The name bedizon'd by the pedant Muse,
The place of fame and elegy supplies,
Who many an L.L.D.— and A.B.—strews,
That bid th' admiring Freshman read and rise.

For who at Hymen's block in youthful bloom,
His scholarship and freedom e'er resign'd,
Left the warm precincts of the common room,
Nor sighing cast one farewell wish behind?

To some dear friend by stealth remembrance flies,
A festive glass the drooping mind requires,
His far-off phiz keen Fancy's eye descries,
Even in his pipe still live the wonted fires;

For me who, mindful of the life I loved,
In these weak lines its happiness relate,
And with fair images of past joys moved
Compare my present with my former state;

Should e'er in future day some roaming friend[4]
(The lions gazing whilst his horses wait)
In breathless speed his steps to Trin. Coll. bend,
And waste an idle question on my fate,

"Haply old Kitt, with iron tears, may say[5]
"To read the lessons oft I've seen the lad,
"Brushing from broken cap the dust away,
"Limp with a paper band across the quad;

"His listless length at breakfast would he lay
"There in that sunless corner cobweb hung,
"Gods, how he crack'd his eggs and drank his tea,
"And pored upon the kettle as it sung!

"Hard by yon gate now painted as in scorn,
"Muttering rude rhymes he stood and fancies wild,
"Rack'd with a dose of salts like one forlorn,
"Or craz'd with duans, or cross'd with bastard child;

"One morn I miss'd him in the chapel train,
"Along the court, and near his well-known fire,
"The eggs were placed, the kettle boil'd in vain,
"No more he came his breakfast to require.

"Next post the tidings came; in due array
"At Hymen's shrine the youth was seen to bend;
"Here may'st thou read, 'tis English all, a lay,
"The farewell tribute of some lonely friend.[6]

1. Mr Pitt's tax upon births.
2. Dr Price upon Population.
3. A club in Oxford of that name, chiefly consisting of noblemen and men of fortune.
4. For the cast of this natural thought the author is indebted to a most inimitable passage in Churchill.
5. The personage here alluded to is no less than the Author's bed-maker, an old soldier much distinguished for his honesty and roughness, and can only be understood by his friends in college.
6. To a most ingenious and valuable friend the author is indebted for the five concluding stanzas of this piece.

110

WILLIAM WORDSWORTH

(1770–1850)

The son of an attorney, born in Cockermouth, Wordsworth was educated at Hawkshead and Cambridge (1787–91). He seems first to have visited Oxford (with his sister Dorothy) in 1798. In 1820 the Wordsworths passed through Oxford on their way to London for a family wedding, and thence to the Continent for a tour which lasted until November. (The 'She' of the second of these poems is Mary, the poet's wife.) One later visit was to receive an honorary DCL in 1839; in the following year, in a letter to Benjamin Robert Haydon, Wordsworth declared, 'I love and honour [Oxford] for abundant reasons; nor can I ever forget the distinction bestowed upon myself last summer by that noble-minded University.'

Oxford, May 30, 1820

Ye sacred Nurseries of blooming Youth!
In whose collegiate shelter England's Flowers
Expand, enjoying through their vernal hours
The air of liberty, the light of truth;
Much have ye suffered from Time's gnawing tooth:
Yet, O ye spires of Oxford! domes and towers!
Gardens and groves! your presence overpowers
The soberness of reason; till, in sooth,
Transformed, and rushing on a bold exchange
I slight my own beloved Cam, to range
Where silver Isis leads my stripling feet;
Pace the long avenue, or glide adown
The stream-like windings of that glorious street—
An eager Novice robed in fluttering gown!

Oxford, May 30, 1820

Shame on this faithless heart! that could allow
Such transport, though but for a moment's space;
Not while—to aid the spirit of the place—
The crescent moon clove with its glittering prow
The clouds, or night-bird sang from shady bough;
But in plain daylight:—She, too, at my side,
Who, with her heart's experience satisfied,
Maintains inviolate its slightest vow!
Sweet Fancy! other gifts must I receive;
Proofs of a higher sovereignty I claim;
Take from *her* brow the withering flowers of eve,
And to that brow life's morning wreath restore;
Let *her* be comprehended in the frame
Of these illusions, or they please no more.

ROBERT SOUTHEY
(1774–1843)

Southey was expelled from Westminster School in 1792 because of his Jacobin sympathies and for an essay against corporal punishment contributed to a magazine he had helped to found, *The Flagellant*. He went up to Balliol College in 1793, where he read widely, swam and rowed, talked and argued, poured out great quantities of verse, rebelled against University rules, and developed some characteristic enthusiasms: 'I have walked over the ruins of Godstow nunnery with sensations such as the site of Troy or Carthage would inspire.' In 1816, however, he looked back and observed that 'my college years were the least beneficial and the least happy of my life.' His first meeting with Coleridge, and their plans to establish a Utopian colony in America, led to his leaving without taking a degree. Southey's prodigious energies were directed into a varied and fertile literary career; though very uneven and sometimes banal, the best of Southey's output, in both prose and verse, is more accomplished than has been generally recognized in our own times. He was made Poet Laureate in 1813—a measure of how far his youthful republicanism had mellowed.

The Chapel Bell

Lo I, the man who from the Muse did ask
    Her deepest notes to swell the Patriot's meeds,
Am now enforced, a far unfitter task,
For cap and gown to leave my minstrel weeds;
    For yon dull tone that tinkles on the air
Bids me lay by the lyre and go to morning prayer.

Oh how I hate the sound! it is the knell
    That still a requiem tolls to Comfort's hour;
And loth am I, at Superstition's bell,
    To quit or Morpheus' or the Muse's bower:
Better to lie and doze, than gape amain,
Hearing still mumbled o'er the same eternal strain.

Thou tedious herald of more tedious prayers,
    Say, dost thou ever summon from his rest
One being wakening to religious cares?
    Or rouse one pious transport in the breast?
Or rather, do not all reluctant creep
To linger out the time in listlessness or sleep?

I love the bell that calls the poor to pray,
    Chiming from village church its cheerful sound,
When the sun smiles on Labour's holy-day,
    And all the rustic train are gather'd round,
Each deftly dizen'd in his Sunday's best,
And pleased to hail the day of piety and rest.

And when, dim shadowing o'er the face of day
    The mantling mists of even-tide rise slow,
As through the forest gloom I wend my way,
    The minster curfew's sullen voice I know,
And pause, and love its solemn toll to hear,
As made by distance soft it dies upon the ear.

Nor with an idle nor unwilling ear
    Do I receive the early passing-bell;
For, sick at heart with many a secret care,
    When I lie listening to the dead man's knell,
I think that in the grave all sorrows cease,
And would full fain recline my head and be at peace.

But thou, memorial of monastic gall!
    What fancy sad or lightsome hast thou given?
Thy vision-scaring sounds alone recall
    The prayer that trembles on a yawn to heaven,
The snuffling, snaffling Fellow's nasal tone,
And Romish rites retain'd, though Romish faith be
        flown.

                                        Oxford, 1793.

114

Written the Winter After the Installation at Oxford, 1793

Toll on, toll on, old Bell! I'll neither pass
The cold and weary hour in heartless rites,
Nor doze away the time. The fire burns bright,
And, bless the maker of this Windsor-Chair!
(Of polish'd cherry, elbow'd, saddle-seated,)
This is the throne of comfort. I will sit
And study here devoutly:. . . not my Euclid, . . .
For Heaven forbid that I should discompose
That Spider's excellent geometry!
I'll study thee, Puss! Not to make a picture,
I hate your canvas cats and dogs and fools,
Themes that disgrace the pencil. Thou shalt give
A moral subject, Puss. Come, look at me, . . .
Lift up thine emerald eyes! Ay, purr away!
For I am praising thee, I tell thee, Puss,
And Cats as well as Kings like flattery.
For three whole days I heard an old Fur-gown
Bepraised, that made a Duke a Chancellor;
Bepraised in prose it was, bepraised in verse;
Lauded in pious Latin to the skies;
Kudos'd egregiously in heathen Greek;
In sapphics sweetly incensed; glorified
In proud alcaics; in hexameters
Applauded to the very Galleries
That did applaud again, whose thunder-claps,
Higher and longer with redoubling peals
Rung, when they heard the illustrious furbelow'd
Heroically in Popean rhyme
Tee-ti-tum'd, in Miltonic blank bemouth'd;
Prose, verse, Greek, Latin, English, rhyme and blank,
Till Eulogy, with all her wealth of words,
Grew bankrupt, all-too-prodigal of praise,
And panting Panegyric toil'd in vain
O'er-task'd in keeping pace with such desert.
Though I can poetize right willingly,
Puss, on thy well-streak'd coat, to that Fur-gown
I was not guilty of a single line:

'Twas an old furbelow, that would hang loose,
And wrap round any one, as it were made
To fit him only, so it were but tied
With a blue riband.
                        What a power there is
In beauty! Within these forbidden walls
Thou hast thy range at will, and when perchance
The Fellows see thee, Puss, they overlook
Inhibitory laws, or haply think
The statute was not made for Cats like thee;
For thou art beautiful as ever Cat
That wanton'd in the joy of kittenhood.
Ay, stretch thy claws, thou democratic beast, . . .
I like thine independence. Treat thee well,
Thou art as playful as young Innocence;
But if we act the governor, and break
The social compact, Nature gave those claws
And taught thee how to use them. Man,
      methinks,
Master and slave alike, might learn from thee
A salutary lesson: but the one
Abuses wickedly his power unjust,
The other crouches spaniel-like, and licks
The hand that strikes him. Wiser animal,
I look at thee, familiarised, yet free;
And, thinking that a child with gentle hand
Leads by a string the large-limb'd Elephant,
With mingled indignation and contempt
Behold his drivers goad the biped beast.

Inscription for a Monument at Oxford

Here Latimer and Ridley in the flames
Bore witness to the truth. If thou hast walk'd
Uprightly through the world, just thoughts of joy
May fill thy breast in contemplating here
Congenial virtue. But if thou hast swerved
From the straight path of even rectitude,
Fearful in trying seasons to assert
The better cause, or to forsake the worse
Reluctant, when perchance therein enthrall'd
Slave to false shame, oh! thankfully receive
The sharp compunctious motions that this spot
May wake within thee, and be wise in time,
And let the future for the past atone.
                                    Bath, 1797.

ANONYMOUS

This epigram redolent of the donnish humour of the early nineteenth century, though not apparently published until much later in the century, reflects on two significant Oxford characters of its time. Cyril Jackson (1746–1819) became Dean of Christ Church in 1783, and proved to be a brilliantly efficient administrator. He held the post until 1809. In 1799 he declined an appointment as Bishop of Oxford, and in 1800 turned down the primacy of Ireland. Nathan Wetherell was Master of University College from 1764 to 1808, and was also Dean of Hereford. Wetherell bought many shares in the Oxford Canal when they were available cheaply and made a considerable fortune as they went up in price. In submitting this epigram to *Notes and Queries*, F. Fitz-Henry says that it was the work of '*Jack* Burton, [who] was then a young lady, daughter of Dr. Burton, a canon of Christ Church, who wrote verses, which were much admired'.

As Cyril and Nathan were walking by Queen's,
Says Cyril to Nathan 'We two are both Deans,
   And Bishops perhaps we shall be!'
Says Nathan 'You may; but as I never shall,
I will take care of my little *canal*,
   And leave you to look for the *See*.'

JOHN KEATS
(1795–1821)

In September and October of 1817 Keats visited his friend
Benjamin Bailey, then an undergraduate at Magdalen Hall;
staying for some five weeks before Michaelmas term began,
Keats worked on *Endymion*, and also wrote these lively lines.
His time in Oxford was, in the words of Robert Gittings,
'of immense formative importance for Keats', his time with
Bailey encouraging him to think deeply and intelligently
about his aims and his nature, as well as stimulating him to read
more widely and systematically than he had hitherto done. In a
letter to his sister Fanny (10 September) he observed: 'This
Oxford I have no doubt is the finest City in the world—it is
full of old Gothic buildings—Spires—towers—Quadrangles—
Cloisters—Groves, etc., and is surrounded with more clear
streams than I ever saw together. I take a Walk by the Side of one
of them every evening and, thank God, we have not had a drop
of rain these many days.'

Lines Rhymed in A Letter From Oxford

The Gothic looks solemn,
The plain Doric column
Supports an old Bishop and Crosier;
The mouldering arch,
Shaded o'er by a larch
Stands next door to Wilson the Hosier.

Vicè—that is, by turns,—
O'er pale faces mourns
The black tasselled trencher and common hat.
The chantry boy sings,
The steeple-bell rings,
And as for the Chancellor—*dominat*.

There are plenty of trees,
And plenty of ease,
And plenty of fat deer for parsons.
And when it is venison,
Short is the benison,
Then each on a leg or thigh fastens.

ROBERT STEPHEN HAWKER

(1803–1875)

Born near Plymouth, Hawker entered Pembroke College in
1823. He won the Newdigate Prize for poetry in 1827 (for a poem
on Pompeii) and was ordained in 1831. From 1844 he was the
energetic (and eccentric) vicar of Morwenstow in Cornwall. He
built a school, restored the church, rebuilt the vicarage, and
shared his parishioners' fascination with the superstitious and
uncanny. He usually dressed in a highly personal manner: his
characteristic costume was described as a cross between a
seaman's outfit and a set of High-Church ecclesiastical robes.
He wrote and published poetry and antiquarian works. His
Quest of the Sangraal (1864) makes a distinctive contribution to
the body of English Arthurian poetry, and some of his ballads,
notably 'The Song of the Western Man' ('And shall Trelawny
die?'), have retained a lasting popularity. He became a Catholic
just twelve hours before his death.

One is Not

There is a cross in Oxford, built of stone,
   They call it there "The Martyrs' Monument;"
   Wise-hearted workmen rear'd it, and they spent
In that proud toil, labour and gold unknown.
   There have they pictur'd many a visible thought
   And deep device, whereby the fathers wrought
Doctrines in walls, and gave dumb roofs a tone.
   Yet, hearken! in yon cloister dim and old,
   They show a simple casket fram'd to hold
An ancient staff. Ye walls of stern Saint John!
   Watch well that relic of the days gone by—
   Thereon Laud lean'd when he went forth to die.
Ha! stout old man, thy fame is still our own,
Though banish'd be thy memory from the graven stone!

THOMAS LOVELL BEDDOES

(1803–1849)

Thomas Lovell Beddoes was the son of Dr Thomas Beddoes, at one time Reader in Chemistry at Oxford, whose patients included Coleridge, Wordsworth, and Southey, whose friends and collaborators included Sir Humphry Davy and James Watt, and whose famous 'pneumatic institute', dedicated to the cure of diseases by the inhalation of gases, was conducted in Bristol from 1798 to 1801. It was in Bristol that the young Beddoes was born, before being educated at Charterhouse and Pembroke College, Oxford. The death of his mother, in Florence, interrupted his degree examinations in 1824. He was awarded an ordinary BA degree in the following year. In 1825 he went to Göttingen as a medical student. He spent the rest of his life in Germany and Switzerland, making only occasional visits to England, including one on which he received his MA at Oxford in April 1828. Receiving his MD from Würzburg in 1831, Beddoes worked as a doctor and also became much involved in subversive political movements. Ever an eccentric, Beddoes was at times in the grip of despair, at others triumphantly happy. He seems to have made several attempts at suicide before eventually killing himself (at the Cigogne Hotel in Basle) by cutting open an artery in his leg. The greater part of his work as a poet and dramatist (mostly much possessed with death) was published posthumously. (The 'knoppe' of line 51 is a 'bud'; lines 68 and 69 allude to one of Drummond of Hawthornden's anecdotes of Ben Jonson: "He hath consumed a whole night in lying looking to his great toe, about which he hath seen Tartars and Turks, Romans and Carthaginians, fight in his imagination".)

Letter to B. W. Procter, Esq. From Oxford; May, 1825

In every tower, that Oxford has, is swung,
Quick, loud, or solemn, the monotonous tongue
Which speaks Time's language, the universal one
After the countenance of moon or sun,—
Translating their still motions to the earth.
I cannot read; the reeling belfry's mirth
Troubles my senses; therefore, Greek, shut up
Your dazzling pages; covered be the cup
Which Homer has beneath his mantle old,

Steamy with boiling life: your petals fold
You fat, square blossoms of the yet young tree
Of Britain-grafted, flourishing Germany:
Hush! Latin, to your grave:—and, with the chime,
My pen shall turn the minutes into rhyme,
And, like the dial, blacken them. There sits,
Or stands, or lounges, or perhaps on bits
Of this rag's daughter, paper, exorcises,
With strange black marks and inky wild devices,
The witch of worlds, the echo of great verse,
About the chasms of the universe,
Ringing and bounding immortality.—
Give him thy bosom, dark Melpomene,
And let him of thy goblet and thine eye
Exhaust the swimming, deep insanity.
He hath the soul, O let it then be fed,
Sea after sea, with that which is not read,
Nor wrung by reasoning from a resolute head,
But comes like lightning on a hill-top steeple;
Heaven's spillings on the lofty laurelled people.
Verse to thee, light to thee, wings upraise thee long
In the unvacillating soar of song,
Thou star-seed of a man! But do not dare
To tempt thy Apollonian god too far,
Clogging and smoking thy young snake, Renown,
In the strait, stony shadows of the town,
Lest he grow weak, and pine, and never be
What he was born, twin to Eternity.
So come, shake London from thy skirts away:
So come, forget not it is England's May.
For Oxford, ho! by moonlight or by sun:
Our horses are not hours, but rather run
Foot by foot faster than the second-sand,
While the old sunteam, like a plough, doth stand
Stuck in thick heaven. Here thou at morn shalt see
Spring's dryad-wakening whisper call the tree,
And move it to green answers; and beneath,
Each side the river which the fishes breathe,
Daisies and grass, whose tops were never stirred,
Or dews made tremulous, but by foot of bird.

And you shall mark in spring's heaven-tapestried room
Yesterday's knoppe, burst by its wild perfume,
Like woman's childhood, to this morning's bloom;
And here a primrose pale beneath a tree,
And here a cowslip longing for its bee,
And violets and lilies every one
Grazing in the great pasture of the sun,
Beam after beam, visibly as the grass
Is swallowed by the lazy cows that pass.
Come look, come walk,—and there shall suddenly
Seize you a rapture and a phantasy;
High over mountain sweeping, fast and high
Through all the intricacies of the sky,
As fast and far a ship-wrecked hoard of gold
Dives ocean, cutting every billow's fold.
These are the honey-minutes of the year
Which make man god, and make a god—Shakespeare.
Come, gather them with me. If not, then go,
And with thee all the ghosts of Jonson's toe,
The fighting Tartars and the Carthaginians:
And may your lady-muse's stiff-winged pinions
Be naked and impossible to fly,
Like a fat goose pen-plucked for poetry.
A curse upon thy cream to make it sour:
A curse upon thy tea-pot every hour;
Spirits of ice possess it! and thy tea,
Changed at its contact, hay and straw leaves be!
A cold and nipping ague on thine urn!
And an invisible canker eat and burn
The mathematic picture, near your fire,
Of the grave, compass-handed, quiet sire!
No more.—Be these the visions of your sorrow
When you have read this doggrel through to-morrow,
And then refuse to let our Oxford borrow
You of the smoky-faced, Augustan town,
And unpersuaded drop the paper down.

ROBERT MONTGOMERY

(1807–1855)

Montgomery was the illegitimate son of a Bath schoolmistress and an actor in the local theatre. Precociously talented and facile, at seventeen he founded a short-lived weekly newspaper, and his first book-length poem was published when he was twenty. In 1828 he published *The Omnipresence of the Deity*, which went into many editions. In 1830 appeared his most famous and popular poem, *Satan, Or Intellect Without God*. The poem found many readers, despite Macaulay's brilliantly destructive review of *The Omnipresence* and *Satan*, published in the *Edinburgh Review*. In the same year, 1830, Montgomery entered Lincoln College and obtained his BA in 1833. Having been ordained in 1835, he worked in chapels in Glasgow and London, proving to be a popular preacher and energetic in his pastoral duties. His later publications included many sermons and poems such as *Luther* (1842) and *Scarborough: a Poetic Glance* (1846). His blank-verse didacticism, so popular in its own time, embodies a taste surely never likely to return.

from *Oxford: Or, Alma Mater*

The Sun is up! behold a princely day,
And all things glorious in its glorious ray;
Ascend the Radcliffe's darkly-winding coil
Of countless steps, nor murmur at the toil;
For lo! a Scene, when that ascension's o'er,
Where none can gaze, nor in that gaze adore,—
There, from the base of her commanding Dome
O'er many a mile the feasting eye may roam,
While music-wing'd, the winds of freshness sound,
Like airy haunters of the region round.
Yon heaven is azured to one dazzling die;
Beneath—a splendor that surpasses eye!
Spire, tow'r, and steeple, roofs of radiant tile,
The costly temple, and collegiate pile,
In sumptuous mass of mingled form and hue,
Await the wonder of thy sateless view.
Far to the west, autumnal meadows wind
Whose fading tints fall tender on the mind;
And near, a hoary tow'r with dial'd side,

And nearer still, in many-window'd pride,
All Souls', with central towers superbly grand;
But see! the clouds are torn,—they break,—expand,
And sunshine, welcomed by each ancient pile,
Like Past and Present when they meet to smile,
With tinting magic beautifully falls
On fretted pinnacles, and fresco'd walls,
Till dark St. Mary, with symmetric spire,
Swells into glory as her shades retire,
And Maudlin trees, that wave o'er Cherwell stream,
Flash on the view and flutter in the beam!
In yellow faintness, lo! that sun-burst dies,
The vision changes with the change of skies;
Again have Cent'ries their dominion won,
As shadows triumph o'er the failing Sun,
Till College grandeur, veil'd in gloom sublime,
Reigns in the darkness that is due to time! . . .

But night is throned; and full before me frown
The dusky Steeples that o'ertop the town;
High in the midst, a dark-domed shadow see,—
The Radcliffe, pile of age-worn majesty;
Around it, silver'd by some window ray
Whirls many a smoke-wreath in ascending play:
Beneath, what massy roofs inmingl'd lie,
Misshaped by fancy, till they awe the eye!
Hush'd are the groves, in leafy dimness veil'd,
The winds unheard, as though they ne'er had rail'd.
But hark! the waving sounds of Wolsey's bell
Float o'er the city like his last farewell,
While answ'ring Temples, with obedient sound,
Peal to the night, and moan sad music round;
But dread o'er all, like thunder heard in dreams,
The warning spirit of that echo seems!
Now gates are barr'd; and, faithful to his stand,
The crusty Porter, with his key-worn hand.

Yet not with day, the day-born studies end;
Wan cheeks, and weary brows,—I see them bend
O'er haughty pages breathing ancient mind,
For Man and Immortality design'd:
The brain may burn, the martyr'd health may fail,
And sunken eyelids speak a mournful tale
Of days protracted into hideous length,
Till mind is dead, and limbs deny their strength!
Still, honours woo!—and may they smile on thee,
Whoe'er thou art, that hop'st their smile to see;
Hours, days, and years, severer far than thine,
In toil, and gloom, and loneliness, are mine! . . .

FREDERICK WILLIAM FABER

(1814–1863)

Born in Yorkshire, son of an Anglican clergyman, Faber was
educated at Shrewsbury School and Harrow; he matriculated at
Balliol in 1832 and went into residence the following year. In
1834 he was elected a Scholar of University College. As an
undergraduate he distinguished himself as a speaker at the
Union, and won the Newdigate Prize of 1836 for his poem on
'The Knights of St. John'. He rapidly developed an admiration
for J. H. Newman. In 1837 he was elected a Fellow of University
College, Oxford and ordained deacon in Ripon Cathedral. After
a period as the rector of Elton in Huntingdonshire from 1842, he
was received into the Catholic Church in 1845 and established a
Catholic community, the 'Wilfridians', he being known as
Brother Wilfrid. From 1849 until his death he was head of the
London Oratory in King William Street in the Strand. In 1854 he
was created DD by Pope Pius IX. Faber's most enduring fame is
through his hymns, such as 'The Land Beyond the Sea' and 'My
God, How Wonderful Thou Art'.

from *Christ-Church Meadow*

I walked within a meadow, where
The willow tops were burnished fair
With cold November's windy gleams,
And watched two green and earthy streams
Along the white frost-beaded grass
With their leaf-laden waters pass.
  And bright rose the towers
  Through the half-stripped bowers,
    And the sun on the windows danced:
  The churches looked white
  In the morning light,
    And the gilded crosses glanced.

Methought as I gazed on yon holy pile,
Statue and moulding and buttress bold
Seemed pencilled with flame, and burning the while
Like the shapes in a furnace of molten gold.
As the fire sank down or glowed anew,
The fretted stones of the fabric grew

So thin that the eye might pierce them through,
Till statue and moulding and buttress bold,
And each well-known figure and carving old,
Peeled off from their place in the turret hoar,
Like the winter bark from a sycamore,
And dropped away as the misty vest
That morning strips from the mountain's breast:
And as the earthly building fell,
    That was so old and strong,
Clear glowed the Church Invisible
    Which had been veiled so long.
And in the midst there rose a Mount,
    The greenest verdure showing;
And from the summit many a fount
    In emerald streaks was flowing,
And each within its mossy bed,
Most like a soft and silver thread,
    In wavy curves was glowing . . .

from *Cherwell: A Descriptive Poem*

In flowery May or shady June
Oft have I spent a vacant noon
In Cherwell's matted hawthorn bowers
Or coves of elder, while the hours
In deep sensations of delight
Sped past me with the silent might
Of time unnoted, which for ever
Sweeps onward like a voiceless river;
And now and then a most sweet thought
Or outward beauty in me wrought
With such blithe trouble as to bring
The noontide's pleasant lingering
Most sensibly unto me: these,
Like the soft shaking of a breeze,
The pulse of summer in the trees,
Were my sole hours, my notes of time,
Joy striking joy, an inward chime

Of silent song, yet not the less
All resonant with cheerfulness.
There, stretched at lazy length, I read,
With boughs of blossom overhead,
And here and there the liquid blue
Of the smooth sky was melting through . . .

O many an evening have I been
Entranced upon that glorious scene,
When silent thought hath proved too strong
For utterance in tranquil song.
There intermingling with the trees
The city rose in terraces
Of radiant buildings, backed with towers
And dusky folds of elm-tree bowers.
St. Mary's watchmen, mute and old,
Each rooted to a buttress bold,
From out their lofty niche looked down
Upon the calm monastic town,
Upon the single glistering dome,
And princely Wykeham's convent home,
And the twin minarets that spring
Like buoyant arrows taking wing,
And square in Moorish fashion wrought
As though from old Granada brought,
And that famed street, whose goodly show
In double crescent lies below,
And Bodley's court, and chestnut bower
    That overhangs the garden wall,
And sheds all day white flakes of flower
    From off its quiet coronal.
Methinks I see it at this hour,—
    How silently the blossoms fall! . . .

EDWARD CASWALL
(1814–1878)

Caswall was born at Yately in Hampshire and educated at Marlborough College before entering Brasenose in 1832. After being ordained he became curate of Stratford-sub-Castle in Wiltshire. This post he resigned and entered the Catholic Church in 1847. He joined Newman's Oratory of St Philip Neri. After some lighthearted early publications, such as his *Sketches of Young Ladies, in which these interesting members of the animal kingdom are classified according to their several instincts, habits and general characteristics* (1837), his writings were devotional in nature. His *Lyra Catholica* of 1849 contains some excellent translations from the Breviary and Missal hymns.

Lines Written on Leaving Oxford

How well I remember the hour,
    When first from the brow of this hill,
I gazed upon spire and tower,
    Becalm'd in the valley so still!

The birds sweetly sang in mine ear,
    Still sweeter sang hope at my heart;
How bright did the prospect appear,
    What thrilling emotions impart!

Since then seven years have expired,
    Seven years which I sigh but to name;
Yet I have more than all I desired
    Of knowledge, of friendship, of fame.

How strange are the feelings of man!
    How changefully link'd with each other!
One feeling is strong when we plan,
    We succeed,—it is turn'd to another.

Oh teach me, great Teacher of all,
    Such wisdom to learn and to love,
So to feel, that whatever befall,
    It may lead me to better above.

There only are destined to bloom
　The hopes that we cherish below;
There the past is divested of gloom;
　No pain can the future bestow.

MATTHEW ARNOLD

(1822–1888)

The son of Thomas Arnold, headmaster of Rugby, Matthew Arnold was born at Laleham, near Staines. He was educated at Winchester, Rugby, and Balliol College, Oxford. His poem on Cromwell won him the Newdigate Prize in 1843; in 1845 he was elected a Fellow of Oriel College. He spent some time (1847–51) as private secretary to Lord Lansdowne, before becoming (in 1851) an inspector of schools; between 1857 and 1867 he was Professor of Poetry at Oxford. His major works of literary and social criticism include *Essays in Criticism* (1865, 1888), *Culture and Anarchy* (1869), *Literature and Dogma* (1872), and *Discourses on America* (1885). His earliest collection of poetry was *The Strayed Reveller and Other Poems* (1849), but he gained no great measure of public attention until *Poems* (1853) appeared.

from *Thyrsis: A Monody, to commemorate the author's friend, Arthur Hugh Clough, who died at Florence, 1861.*

How changed is here each spot man makes or fills!
   In the two Hinkseys nothing keeps the same;
      The village-street its haunted mansion lacks,
   And from the sign is gone Sibylla's name,
      And from the roofs the twisted chimney-stacks;
         Are ye too changed, ye hills?
See, 'tis no foot of unfamiliar men
   Tonight from Oxford up your pathway strays
   Here came I often, often, in old days;
Thyrsis and I; we still had Thyrsis then.

Runs it not here, the track by Childworth Farm,
   Up past the wood, to where the elm-tree crowns
      The hill behind whose ridge the sunset flames?
   The signal-elm, that looks on Ilsley Downs,
      The Vale, the three lone weirs, the youthful
         Thames?—
         This winter-eve is warm,
Humid the air; leafless, yet soft as spring,
   The tender purple spray on copse and briers;
   And that sweet City with her dreaming spires,
She needs not June for beauty's heightening,

132

Lovely all times she lies, lovely to-night!
   Only, methinks, some loss of habit's power
      Befalls me wandering through this upland dim;
   Once pass'd I blindfold here, at any hour,
      Now seldom come I, since I came with him.
         That single elm-tree bright
   Against the west—I miss it! is it gone?
      We prized it dearly; while it stood, we said,
      Our friend, the Scholar-Gipsy, was not dead;
   While the tree lived, he in these fields lived on.

Too rare, too rare, grow now my visits here!
   But once I knew each field, each flower, each stick;
      And with the country-folk acquaintance made
   By barn in threshing-time, by new-built rick.
      Here, too, our shepherd-pipes we first assay'd.
         Ah me! this many a year
   My pipe is lost, my shepherd's-holiday!
      Needs must I lose them, needs with heavy heart
      Into the world and wave of men depart;
   But Thyrsis of his own will went away . . .

GEORGE WALTER THORNBURY
(1828–1876)

Born in London, Thornbury worked as a journalist, popular historian, biographer, and versifier. He was associated with Dickens as a contributor to *All the Year Round* and *Household Words*. He was a prolific travel writer, publishing accounts of journeys made in the USA, Palestine, Turkey, and elsewhere. He wrote an interesting *Life of J. M. W Turner* (1861).

Smith of Maudlin

My chums will burn their Indian weeds
   The very night I pass away,
And cloud-propelling puff and puff,
   As white the thin smoke melts away;
Then Jones of Wadham, eyes half-closed,
   Rubbing the ten hairs on his chin,
Will say, "This very pipe I use
   Was poor old Smith's of Maudlin."

That night in High Street there will walk
   The ruffling gownsmen three abreast,
The stiff-necked proctors, wary-eyed,
   The dons, the coaches, and the rest;
Sly "Cherub Sims" will then purpose
   Billiards, or some sweet ivory sin;
Tom cries, "He played a pretty game—
   Did honest Smith of Maudlin."

The boats are out!—the arrowy rush,
   The mad bull's jerk, the tiger's strength;
The Balliol men have wopped the Queen's—
   Hurrah! but only by a length.
Dig on, ye muffs; ye cripples, dig!
   Pull blind, till crimson sweats the skin;—
The man who bobs and steers cries, "Oh
   For plucky Smith of Maudlin!"

Wine-parties met—a noisy night,
   Red sparks are breaking through the cloud;
The man who won the silver cup
   Is in the chair erect and proud;
Three are asleep—one to himself
   Sings, "Yellow jacket's sure to win."
A silence:—"Men, the memory
   Of poor old Smith of Maudlin!"

The boxing-rooms—with solemn air
   A freshman dons the swollen glove;
With slicing strokes the lapping sticks
   Work out a rubber—three and love;
With rasping jar the padded man
   Whips Thompson's foil, so square and thin,
And cries, "Why, zur, you've not the wrist
   Of Muster Smith of Maudlin."

But all this time beneath the sheet
   I shall lie still, and free from pain,
Hearing the bed-makers sluff in
   To gossip round the blinded pane;
Try on my rings, sniff up my scent,
   Feel in my pockets for my tin;
While one hag says, "We all must die,
   Just like this Smith of Maudlin."

Ah! then a dreadful hush will come,
   And all I hear will be the fly
Buzzing impatient round the wall,
   And on the sheet where I must lie;
Next day a jostling of feet—
   The men who bring the coffin in:
"This is the door—the third-pair back,—
   Here's Mr. Smith of Maudlin!"

EDWIN ARNOLD

(1832–1904)

Arnold, the son of a Sussex magistrate, was a Scholar of
University College; as an undergraduate he won the Newdigate
Prize for a poem on Belshazzar's feast. Work as a schoolteacher
took him to Poona in India. After his return to England in 1861,
he became a journalist and was later editor of the *Daily Telegraph*.
His extensive work as a poet was largely devoted to the
presentation of Oriental thought and life, most famously in *The
Light of Asia* (1879), a verse account of the Buddha's life and
teaching.

Oxford Revisited

Mother! mild Mother! after many years—
   So many that the head I bow turns grey—
   Come I once more to thee, thinking to say
In what far lands, through what hard hopes and fears,
'Mid how much toil and triumph, joys and tears
   I taught thy teaching; and, withal, to lay
   At thy kind feet such of my wreaths as may
Seem least unworthy. But what grown child dares
Offer thee honours, Fair and Queenly One!
   Tower-crowned, and girdled with thy silver streams,
Mother of ah! so many a better son?
   Let me but list thy solemn voice, which seems
   Like Christ's, raising my dead: and let me be
   Back for one hour—a Boy—beside thy knee.
                      May 1883.

THEODORE WATTS-DUNTON

(1832–1914)

Watts-Dunton was born at St Ives in Huntingdonshire. Educated privately, he later settled and worked in London. He established himself as an influential reviewer of poetry on the *Athenæum* and the *Examiner*. His volume of poems *The Coming of Love* was very well received on its publication in 1897, as was his romance *Aylwin* in the next year. The article on 'Poetry' which he contributed to the ninth edition of the *Encylopaedia Britannica* (1885) remains well worth reading. Watts-Dunton acted as a guardian of sorts to Swinburne (the 'A. C. S.' of 'The Last Walk From Boar's Hill'); from 1879 Swinburne lived in Watts-Dunton's house in Putney. Benjamin Jowett, Master of Balliol, who makes an important appearance in Watts-Dunton's poem, continued to stimulate poets even after his death; see, for example, John Wain's 'At Jowett's Grave' in his *Poems 1949–1979* (1980).

The Last Walk From Boar's Hill. To A. C. S.

I

One after one they go; and glade and heath,
   Where once we walked with them, and garden
     bowers
   They made so dear, are haunted by the hours
Once musical of those who sleep beneath;
One after one does Sorrow's every wreath
   Bind closer you and me with funeral flowers,
   And Love and Memory from each loss of ours
Forge conquering glaives to quell the conqueror Death.

Since Love and Memory now refuse to yield
The friend with whom we walk through mead and field
   To-day as on that day when last we parted,
Can he be dead, indeed, whatever seem?
Love shapes a presence out of Memory's dream,
   A living presence, Jowett golden-hearted.

II

Can he be dead? We walk through flowery ways
   From Boar's Hill down to Oxford, fain to know
   What nugget-gold, in drift of Time's long flow,
The Bodleian mine hath stored from richer days;
He, fresh as on that morn, with sparkling gaze,
   Hair bright as sunshine, white as moonlit snow,
   Still talks of Plato while the scene below
Breaks gleaming through the veil of sunlit haze.

Can he be dead? He shares our homeward walk,
And by the river you arrest the talk
   To see the sun transfigure ere he sets
The boatmen's children shining in the wherry
   And on the floating bridge the ply-rope wets,
Making the clumsy craft an angel's ferry.

III

The river crossed, we walk 'neath glowing skies
   Through grass where cattle feed or stand and stare
   With burnished coats, glassing the coloured air—
Fading as colour after colour dies:
We pass the copse; we round the leafy rise—
   Start many a coney and partridge, hern and hare;
   We win the scholar's nest—his simple fare
Made royal-rich by welcome in his eyes.

Can he be dead? His heart was drawn to you.
Ah! well that kindred heart within him knew
   The poet's heart of gold that gives the spell!
Can he be dead? Your heart being drawn to him,
How shall ev'n Death make that dear presence dim
   For you who loved him—us who loved him well?

FREDERICK WILLIAM ORDE WARD

(1843–1922)

The son of a clergyman, Ward was born at Blendworth in Hampshire and educated at Tonbridge School and Wadham College, Oxford, where he obtained his BA in 1865. He worked as a private tutor in Oxford and was then ordained in 1868. Some of his work was published under the pseudonym of Frederick Harald Williams. His *Selected Poems* was published posthumously in 1924.

To the Bodleian Librarian

Friend, suckled with me at the same rude fount,
   Rough as the fabled Roman she-wolf's breast,
While taught with me to climb the classic mount
   And drink the waters of a wild unrest.
Ah, the fierce rapture of that sacred stream
   Poured in thy heart and hospitable mind
The passion and the glory of a dream,
   And all the freedom of the ocean wind;
And thou hast won this vision for thy own,
   Though I but humbly gaze on it from far,
And passed through spaces yet unmapt, unknown,
   Beyond the footstep of the last faint star.

Now crownèd as a king among thy books
   Thou sittest calm while subjects urge their plea,
As a great rock that marks a thousand brooks
   Go babbling on down to the silent sea;
Innumerable servants round thee range
   And welcome are in every human speech,
That note the fevered pulse of party change
   Or troubled tide of reason's utmost reach;
And all the thought of all the boundless earth
   Before thee spreads the riches of its stores,
The secret of the air, the dew and dearth,
   And the dim murmur of untravelled shores.

Each day to thee a hundred vassals bear
    Their gold and spices, and the precious gems
Fit for the monarchs of the mind to wear
    And to adorn the sages' diadems;
The softest ripple of the farthest ray
    Just wafted to thee with its joy unspent,
The song that dazzles for a summer day,
    The thunder of a nation's argument,
The breath that trembles upon maiden lips,
    The blushing of the blossom at her feet,
The tempest wrought of earthquake and eclipse,
    In the grand cycle of the ages meet.

Electric lines through all the seas and lands,
    Where reignest thou in study long and lone,
Obey the touch of thy compelling hands
    And bind the world as subject to thy throne;
The treasures of the height and of the deep,
    The flowers that sparkle on the breast of night,
Unfold to thee in thy majestic sweep
    The inner sweetness of their hidden sight;
Oh, thou hast glimpses there of Nature nude
    And treadest where but veiled the angels dare,
In uncompanioned awful solitude
    Beneath the shadow of imperial care.

GERARD MANLEY HOPKINS

(1844–1889)

Hopkins was born at Stratford in Essex, the son of a well-to-do marine insurance agent. He attended Highgate School before entering Balliol in April 1863. In a letter to his parents he reported that 'everything is delightful, I have met with much attention and am perfectly comfortable. Balliol is the friendliest and snuggest of colleges, our inner quad is delicious and has a grove of fine trees and lawns where bowls are the order of the evening.' (In 1865 he wrote two sonnets 'To Oxford'.) In 1866 he converted to Catholicism, became a Jesuit novice two years later, and was ordained in 1877. In November 1878 he returned to Oxford as curate of St Aloysius's church, but stayed there less than a year ('Duns Scotus's Oxford' and 'Binsey Poplars' were both written during this period) before being moved first to Manchester and then Liverpool. From 1882 to 1884 he taught at Stonyhurst College, before becoming Professor of Greek at University College, Dublin.

Duns Scotus's Oxford

Towery city and branchy between towers;
Cuckoo-echoing, bell-swarmèd, lark-charmèd, rook
   racked, river-rounded;
The dapple-eared lily below thee; that country and town
   did
Once encounter in, here coped and poisèd powers;

Thou hast a base and brickish skirt there, sours
That neighbour-nature thy grey beauty is grounded
Best in; graceless growth, thou hast confounded
Rural rural keeping—folk, flocks, and flowers.

Yet ah! this air I gather and I release
He lived on; these weeds and waters, these walls are what
He haunted who of all men most sways my spirits to
   peace;

Of realty the rarest-veinèd traveller; a not
Rivalled insight, be rival Italy or Greece;
Who fired France for Mary without spot.

Binsey Poplars

My aspens dear, whose airy cages quelled,
Quelled or quenched in leaves the leaping sun,
All felled, felled, are all felled;
   Of a fresh and following folded rank
       Not spared, not one
       That dandled a sandalled
     Shadow that swam or sank
On meadow and river and wind-wandering weed-
   winding bank.
O if we but knew what we do
       When we delve or hew—
    Hack and rack the growing green!
      Since country is so tender
   To touch, her being só slender,
   That, like this sleek and seeing ball
   But a prick will make no eye at all,
     Where we, even where we mean
       To mend her we end her,
     When we hew or delve:
After-comers cannot guess the beauty been.
   Ten or twelve, only ten or twelve
     Strokes of havoc únselve
       The sweet especial scene,
     Rural scene, a rural scene,
     Sweet especial rural scene.

FRANCIS WILLIAM BOURDILLON

(1852–1921)

Bourdillon was a Scholar of Worcester College. For three years from 1876 he was resident tutor, at Cumberland Lodge, to the two sons of Prince and Princess Christian. He later lived in Eastbourne and tutored private pupils for University entrance. The Latin epigraph to the second of these poems might be translated thus: "For thus by your own testimony you stand condemned: for you are the sons of those who slaughtered the prophets".

Port Meadow, Oxford

O wide wan waste of waters, where no breath
Ruffles the mirror surface, but the gray
   Of clouds above is real as if the day
Were no less gloomy to a world beneath!
O dreary waste, the mind remembereth
   Full many an hour of summer life and play,
   Where now beneath is lifeless slime and clay,
And the vast level lies like ashen death.

Yet as at eve on the wild scene I pondered,
   While thoughts of horror held my pulses hushed,
   Sudden, amid the clouds beneath that rushed,
Shone out a star. Ah! would mine eyes have wandered,
   Were there no waters, to that star above?
   Were there no death, should we know all of love?

The Shelley Memorial (in University College, Oxford)

*Itaque testimonio estis vobismet ipsis: quod filii
estis eorum qui prophetas occiderunt.*

This is not Shelley—this dead mask of Death!
   Here is no marble Immortality,
But fleshly petrifaction. Could the breath
   Come back to this, yet nevermore should he,
The stately spirit of full stature, deign
In this small corpse to lodge, and live again.

This is not Shelley! Have our eyes not seen
  Shelley, the child of morning, with the light
Of Heaven about him, and a brow serene
  As Orient noonday, smile on Death and Night,
As the unhappy sisters of man's sorrow,
That might not live to the bright human morrow?

His marble but records Death's victory
  In Death's own lying language; who doth boast
That o'er all Being he hath empery,
  And nothing liveth when the breath is lost.
So cold, so white, he cries, your Shelley lay!
Such lifeless limbs! Such heavy soul-less clay!

Where is his Immortality—ah, where?
  Is this the sky of Shelley? These his stars?
This small blue dome, as low, as near, as bare
  As infant man believed it, and these sparse
Gold spangles! Could ye mock our Shelley more
'Twixt him and Heav'n than draw this tinsel o'er?

Yet who here standing blames the sculptor's art?
  So deftly moulded is each marble limb!
Such deathly languor lies on every part!
  So like is this to what was left of him,
When the wave-wantons, tiring of a prey
Teased vainly, flung the emptied flesh away!

Not his the fault, the sculptor's! Is it ours,
  Who leave no more to Art her old domain
Of Fancy, and though sky and sea she scours,
  No more allow her to present us plain
Her aery visions, or to unseen things
Lend bodies visible and birdlike wings?

She bears Egyptian bondage, set to make
  No likeness but what workman souls may see
And test by finger-touch—the fowler's lake,
  The fisher's river-side, the woodman's tree,
The face in soul-less hours of common life,
The body naked for the surgeon's knife.

144

Where are her ancient glories, when to man
　　She brought a revelation all divine,
And opened his dull eyes, and bade him scan
　　Shy Nature, to discern why she did shine,
For all her sorrows, with so calm a light;
And, through the outward, woke the inward sight?

Here had the Greek made plain in mortal form
　　The seed of the Immortals, the half-god;
Here had the Florentine shewn flesh all warm
　　With mystic fire-tints from the Rose of God;
The rudest missal-scribe, his rough child-way,
Had drawn the soul-shape 'scaping from the clay.

We only, lords of lightning and of light,
　　All Nature's magic working to our wand,
Are yet forbidden the most simple sight
　　Of the informing soul in sea or land,
In hills and clouds and the blue deeps above,
And woman's beauty, and the face we love.

One was there, son of England, whom not yet
　　The dust of years hides deeply, who perchance
With visionary touch had made forget
　　This dead marred body, left but to enhance
The bright miraculous likeness upward drawn,
The unprisoned spirit springing to the Dawn.

But Blake, the last Prometheus, is no more,
　　And the dark Heaven has shut her gates again.
Turn to the sleeper here, if in the lore
　　He left us we may find some balm for pain,
May find him living, though this gray-hued Death
So grimly to his dying witnesseth.

There do we find him, with his young-god's face
　　For ever to the East—for ever sure
Of the delaying sunrise, and the grace
　　To dawn upon the dark earth, full and pure
And holy, though a hundred such as he
Should die in faith before that day shall be.

OSCAR FINGALL O'FLAHERTIE WILLS WILDE

(1854–1900)

Born in Dublin, Wilde was educated at Portora Royal School in Enniskillen, Trinity College, Dublin, and Magdalen College, Oxford. While at Oxford (he matriculated in 1874) he won the Newdigate Prize (1878) for his poem 'Ravenna' and in the same year he took a first class degree in *Literae Humaniores*. In 1881 he published his *Poems*, and in the following year travelled to the USA on a lecture tour. His novel, *The Picture of Dorian Gray*, was published in 1891 and in the next three years his plays *Lady Windermere's Fan*, *A Woman of No Importance*, and *The Importance of being Earnest* enjoyed much success. In 1895 he was sentenced to two years' hard labour after being found guilty of homosexual practices. Shortly before his death, Wilde declared that 'the two great turning points in my life were when my father sent me to Oxford, and when society sent me to prison.' (Itys was the son of Procne and Tereus; Tereus raped Philomela, sister of Procne, and cut out her tongue. In revenge Procne killed Itys and served the body to her husband. When he, in his turn, sought revenge, Procne was changed into a nightingale, mourning eternally for her son; Philomela was transformed into a swallow. In many later versions of the myth it is Philomela who (as here) is netamorphosed into a nightingale- "the brown bird".)

Magdalen Walks

The little white clouds are racing over the sky,
 And the fields are strewn with the gold of the flower
  of March,
The daffodil breaks under foot, and the tasselled larch
Sways and swings as the thrush goes hurrying by.

A delicate odour is borne on the wings of the morning
 breeze,
 The odour of deep wet grass, and of brown's new
  furrowed earth,
 The birds are singing for joy of the Spring's glad birth,
Hopping from branch to branch on the rocking trees.

146

And all the woods are alive with the murmur and sound
    of Spring,
    And the rosebud breaks into pink on the climbing
      briar,
    And the crocus-bed is a quivering moon of fire
Girdled round with the belt of an amethyst ring.

And the plane to the pine-tree is whispering some tale of
    love
    Till it rustles with laughter and tosses its mantle of
      green,
    And the gloom of the wych-elm's hollow is lit with the
      iris sheen
Of the burnished rainbow throat and the silver breast of
    a dove.

See! the lark starts up from his bed in the meadow there,
    Breaking the gossamer threads and the nets of dew,
    and flashing a-down the river, a flame of blue!
The kingfisher flies like an arrow, and wounds the air.

from *The Burden Of Itys*

The harmless rabbit gambols with its young
    Across the trampled towing-path, where late
A troop of laughing boys in jostling throng
    Cheered with their noisy cries the racing eight;
The gossamer, with ravelled silver threads,
Works at its little loom, and from the dusky red-eaved
    sheds
Of the lone Farm a flickering light shines out
    Where the swinked shepherd drives his bleating flock
Back to their wattled sheep-cotes, a faint shout
    Comes from some Oxford boat at Sandford lock,
And starts the moor-hen from the sedgy rill,
And the dim lengthening shadows flit like swallows up
    the hill.

The heron passes homeward to the mere,
    The blue mist creeps among the shivering trees,
Gold world by world the silent stars appear,
    And like a blossom blown before the breeze
A white moon drifts across the shimmering sky,
Mute arbitress of all thy sad, thy rapturous threnody.

She does not heed thee, wherefore should she heed,
    She knows Endymion is not far away,
'T is I, 't is I, whose soul is as the reed
    Which has no message of its own to play,
So pipes another's bidding, it is I,
Drifting with every wind on the wide sea of misery.

Ah! the brown bird has ceased: one exquisite trill
    About the sombre woodland seems to cling
Dying in music, else the air is still,
    So still that one might hear the bat's small wing
Wander and wheel above the pines, or tell
Each tiny dew-drop dripping from the bluebell's
        brimming cell.

And far away across the lengthening wold,
    Across the willowy flats and thickets brown,
Magdalen's tall tower tipped with tremulous gold
    Marks the long High Street of the little town,
And warns me to return; I must not wait,
Hark! 't is the curfew booming from the bell at Christ
        Church gate . . .

HENRY CHARLES BEECHING

(1859–1919)

Educated at the City of London School and Balliol, where he was a Classical Exhibitioner, Beeching began his clerical career as curate of Mossley Hill Church in Liverpool (1882–85) and was later a Canon of Westminster Abbey (1902–11) before becoming Dean of Norwich in 1911. He was Professor of Pastoral Theology at King's College, London, from 1900 to 1903. His publications include sermons and other theological writings, poems, and scholarly works and editions of Herbert, Vaughan, and Tennyson. (The subject of the second of Beeching's epigrams later became better known as Sidney Lee, Shakespearean biographer and editor of the *Dictionary of National Biography*.)

On Benjamin Jowett, Master of Balliol

First come I. My name is Jowett.
There's no knowledge but I know it.
I am Master of this College,
What I don't know isn't knowledge.

On Solomon Lazarus Lee, Exhibitioner of Balliol

I am featly-tripping Lee,
Learned in modern history,
My gown, the wonder of beholders
Hangs like a foot-note from my shoulders.

Epilogue

O Mother Oxford, unto whom we cry
   Through all the passing loves and light desires
   Of changing seasons; whom the toil that tires,
The years that sever, and the griefs that sigh,
Have no dominion over; who dost lie
   Ever serene and fair, when morning fires
   Thy silent pinnacles, or when thy spires
Stand flush'd with sunset in the evening sky:
Take in this dark November bare of flowers
   Rough gleanings from the plashy meadow lands,
     Not that our song but that thy face is sweet;
So be that for thy sake, if not for ours,
   May find their place in no unkindly hands
     These gifts we lay, O Mother, at thy feet.

CECIL SPRING-RICE

(1859–1918)

Educated at Eton and Balliol, Spring-Rice went on to a
distinguished career in the diplomatic service, which included
spells as First Secretary of the Embassy in Petrograd (1903–05),
Minister and Consul-General in Persia (1906–08), Minister to
Sweden (1908–12), and British Ambassador to the USA from
1912. A collection of his pleasantly accomplished verse was
published after his death (*Poems*, 1920).

On Henry George Liddell, Dean of Christ Church

I am the Dean of Christ Church, Sir,
This is my wife—look well at her.
She is the Broad: I am the High:
We are the University.

EDITH NESBIT

(1858–1924)

Born in London, Nesbit was educated in France (at an Ursuline convent), Germany, and Brighton. As a girl she was acquainted with the Rossettis, William Morris, and Swinburne. As an adult, a convinced socialist, she moved in the circles of Wells and Shaw; her *Ballads and Lyrics of Socialism* was published in 1908. Unconventional in dress and behaviour, she and her husband, Hubert Bland, were founding members of the Fabian Society. She was a prolific author in many fields, her writings the main financial support of a family which included a number of her husband's illegitimate children. She wrote ghost stories for adults (e.g. *Grim Tales and Something Wrong*, 1893); Gothic romance (e.g. *The Secret of Kyriels*, 1899); domestic fiction (e.g. *The Lark*, 1922), and, most enduringly, stories for children (e.g. *The Treasure Seekers*, 1899; *The Railway Children*, 1908; *The Psammead or Five Children and It*, 1902). The woman who had known Dante Gabriel Rossetti counted Noel Coward among her acquaintances at the end of her life. Robert Bridges's 'College Garden in 1917' offers more solemn meditations on a related subject, and Francis Warner's poem of 1991, 'Inscribed in a Copy of *Oxford and Cambridge Gardens* by Mavis Batey' (in his collection, *Nightingales*, 1997) well illustrates the continuing tradition of poems on college gardens.

New College Gardens, Oxford

On this old lawn, where lost hours pass
　　Across the shadows dark with dew,
Where autumn on the thick sweet grass
　　Has laid a weary leaf or two,
When the young morning, keenly sweet,
　　Breathes secrets to the silent air,
Happy is he whose lingering feet
　　May wander lonely there.

The enchantment of the dreaming limes,
　　The magic of the quiet hours,
Breathe unheard tales of other times
　　And other destinies than ours;

The feet that long ago walked here
    Still, noiseless, walk beside our feet,
Poor ghosts, who found this garden dear,
    And found the morning sweet!

Age weeps that it no more may hold
    The heart-ache that youth clasps so close,
Pain finely shaped in pleasure's mould,
    A thorn deep hidden in a rose.
Here is the immortal thorny rose
    That may in no new garden grow—
Its root is in the hearts of those
    Who walked here long ago.

LIONEL PIGOT JOHNSON
(1867–1902)

The son of an infantry captain, Johnson was educated at Winchester and matriculated at New College in 1886, having won a Scholarship the previous year. He gained a first in *Literae Humaniores* in 1890. After graduating he settled in London and contributed extensively to the journals, in part because of a pressing need to pay off the debts he had incurred at Oxford. In 1891 he became a Catholic. He was much interested in Irish matters, and was a passionate supporter of the Home Rule movement. In his first years in London he mixed extensively in literary circles; his friends included Dowson and Yeats and he introduced Wilde to Alfred Douglas. Soon, however, his habits became increasingly solitary and reclusive. A slight and frail man, never robust, he undermined his health further by his increasingly heavy drinking. His best poems (Yeats called his work 'marmorean') made an important contribution to the poetry of the 1890s.

Oxford Nights

To Victor Plarr.

About the august and ancient *Square*,
Cries the wild wind; and through the air,
The blue night air, blows keen and chill:
Else, all the night sleeps, all is still.
Now, the lone *Square* is blind with gloom:
Now, on that clustering chestnut bloom,
A cloudy moonlight plays, and falls
In glory upon *Bodley*'s walls:
Now, wildlier yet, while moonlight pales,
Storm the tumultuary gales.
O rare divinity of Night!
Season of undisturbed delight:
Glad interspace of day and day!
Without, an world of winds at play:
Within, I hear what dead friends say.
Blow, winds! and round that perfect *Dome*,
Wail as you will, and sweep, and roam:

Above *Saint Mary*'s carven home,
Struggle, and smite to your desire
The sainted watchers on her spire:
Or in the distance vex your power
Upon mine own *New College* tower:
You hurt not these! On me and mine,
Clear candlelights in quiet shine:
My fire lives yet! nor have I done
With *Smollett*, nor with *Richardson*:
With, gentlest of the martyrs! *Lamb*,
Whose lover I, long lover, am:
With *Gray*, whose gracious spirit knew
The sorrows of art's lonely few:
With *Fielding*, great, and strong, and tall;
Sterne, exquisite, equivocal;
Goldsmith, the dearest of them all:
While *Addison*'s demure delights
Turn *Oxford*, into *Attic*, nights.
Still *Trim* and *Parson Adams* keep
Me better company, than sleep:
Dark sleep, who loves not me; nor I
Love well her nightly death to die,
And in her haunted chapels lie.
Sleep wins me not: but from his shelf
Brings me each wit his very self:
Beside my chair the great ghosts throng,
Each tells his story, sings his song:
And in the ruddy fire I trace
The curves of each *Augustan* face.
I sit at *Doctor Primrose'* board:
I hear *Beau Tibbs* discuss a lord.
Mine, *Matthew Bramble*'s pleasant wrath;
Mine, all the humours of the *Bath*.
Sir Roger and the *Man in Black*
Bring me the *Golden Ages* back.
Now white *Clarissa* meets her fate,
With virgin will inviolate:
Now *Lovelace* wins me with a smile,
Lovelace, adorable and vile.
I taste, in slow alternate way,

155

Letters of *Lamb*, letters of *Gray*:
Nor lives there, beneath *Oxford* towers,
More joy, than in my silent hours.
Dream, who love dreams! forget all grief:
Find, in sleep's nothingness, relief:
Better my dreams! Dear, human books,
With kindly voices, winning looks!
Enchaunt me with your spells of art,
And draw me homeward to your heart:
Till weariness and things unkind
Seem but a vain and passing wind:
Till the gray morning slowly creep
Upward, and rouse the birds from sleep:
Till *Oxford* bells the silence break,
And find me happier, for your sake.
Then, with the dawn of common day,
Rest you! But I, upon my way,
What the fates bring, will cheerlier do,
In days not yours, through thoughts of you!

1890.

Oxford

To Arthur Galton.

Over, the four long years! And now there rings
One voice of freedom and regret: *Farewell*!
Now old remembrance sorrows, and now sings:
But song from sorrow, now, I cannot tell.

City of weathered cloister and worn court;
Gray city of strong towers and clustering spires:
Where art's fresh loveliness would first resort;
Where lingering art kindled her latest fires.

Where on all hands, wondrous with ancient grace,
Grace touched with age, rise works of goodliest men:
Next Wykeham's art obtain their splendid place
The zeal of Inigo, the strength of Wren.

156

Where at each coign of every antique street,
A memory hath taken root in stone:
There, Raleigh shone; there, toiled Franciscan feet;
There, Johnson flinched not, but endured, alone.

There, Shelley dreamed his white Platonic dreams;
There, classic Landor throve on Roman thought;
There, Addison pursued his quiet themes;
There, smiled Erasmus, and there, Colet taught.

And there, O memory more sweet than all!
Lived he, whose eyes keep yet our passing light;
Whose crystal lips Athenian speech recall;
Who wears Rome's purple with least pride, most right.

That is the Oxford, strong to charm us yet:
Eternal in her beauty and her past.
What, though her soul be vexed? She can forget
Cares of an hour: only the great things last.

Only the gracious air, only the charm,
And ancient might of true humanities:
These, nor assault of man, nor time, can harm;
Not these, nor Oxford with her memories.

Together have we walked with willing feet
Gardens of plenteous trees, bowering soft lawn:
Hills, whither Arnold wandered; and all sweet
June meadows, from the troubling world withdrawn:

Chapels of cedarn fragrance, and rich gloom
Poured from empurpled panes on either hand:
Cool pavements, carved with legends of the tomb;
Grave haunts, where we might dream, and understand.

Over, the four long years! And unknown powers
Call to us, going forth upon our way:
Ah! turn we, and look back upon the towers,
That rose above our lives, and cheered the day.

Proud and serene, against the sky, they gleam:
Proud and secure, upon the earth, they stand:
Our city hath the air of a pure dream,
And hers indeed is an Hesperian land.

Think of her so! the wonderful, the fair,
The immemorial, and the ever young:
The city, sweet with our forefathers' care;
The city, where the Muses all have sung.

Ill times may be; she hath no thought of time:
She reigns beside the waters yet in pride.
Rude voices cry: but in her ears the chime
Of full, sad bells brings back her old springtide.

Like to a queen in pride of place, she wears
The splendour of a crown in Radcliffe's dome.
Well fare she, well! As perfect beauty fares;
And those high places, that are beauty's home.
                                        1890.

ANONYMOUS

(fl.1894)

The Don Fin de Siècle

The days of port and peace are gone,
I am a modern Oxford Don;
No more I haunt the candled gloom,
The cosy chairs of Common-Room;
No more the senior man discourses,
Of wine, of women fair and horses,
Tells with cracked voice and mellow pride
Old stories of the covert-side,
Or with sad sighs dim forms recalls
Whose grey slabs line the cloister walls.
Student and hunter both are fled,
All their age is "lapped in lead."
Each day the peal of marriage bells
Tradition's gathered mist dispels;
Our life's more complex daily grown,
And no man calls his soul his own.
Myself, a man of modest mark,
Make my snug nest beyond the Park,
Pay twice the rent my means afford,
Spread the too hospitable board,
And take each post the gods will give
To multiply the ways to live.
Each new device earns hearty greeting;
I lecture to the Summer Meeting;
Of each new school I know the ways
And keep in touch with each new craze.
No time for learning (Ah the pity!)
I spend whole days upon Committee;
Vacation takes a reading party
To Marazion or Cromarty.
On every stage of life I'm seen,
At Toynbee Hall or Bethnal Green;
To-day for County Council standing,
To-morrow Volunteers commanding;
The time I spare from Caucus voting

I give to Company promoting,
Write leaders for the "Daily Rag"
and pen cheap satire for the "Mag.,"
My soul from donnishness deliver
And feign a passion for the river;
With wise discretion spare the rod
And build the bonfire in the quad.
With borrowed lights from Teuton lore,
The past, the future I explore;
And make an easy reputation
By drafts on that laborious nation.
In Wren I see the source of evil,
Do my own coaching for the "Civil,"
With good spoon-meat (heaven help the fools!)
I feed my pupils for the Schools:
Choked with the stodgy stuff I cram in 'em,
They face their fate and I examine 'em,
Devise new ways to find them out
And my own labours lightly flout.
Meanwhile, the long-expected tome,
"Plato", "Thucydides" or "Rome,"
The book to justify my claim
To Thinker's or Historian's name,
As Horace bids, suppressed nine years,
Ever appearing ne'er appears;
When the fine fruit of toil is ripe,
At last emerges from the type
The small edition (hardy annual!)
The "Outline" or "Extension Manual,"
For Cambridge scoff or German jest,
Ohne Bedeutung at the best.
"And what's the end?" Ah, there's the riddle,
I break my sermon in the middle.

JAMES ELROY FLECKER
(1884–1915)

Flecker was born at Lewisham in London and attended Dean Close School in Cheltenham (where his father was headmaster), followed by Uppingham and Trinity College, Oxford. He was in Oxford from 1902 to 1907. Seeking a post in the Consular Service, he studied Oriental languages in Cambridge. He was sent to Constantinople in June of 1910, where he began to show signs of serious ill-health. He was later posted to Smyrna and Beirut. As his health deteriorated, he spent the last eighteen months of his life in Switzerland. His first collection of poems, *The Bridge of Fire*, was published in 1907. His drama *Hassan* was staged in 1923. For a different response to the Oxford Canal, see E. J. Scovell's 'The Canal' (*Selected Poems*, 1991).

Oxford Canal

When you have wearied of the valiant spires of this
    County Town,
Of its wide white streets and glistening museums, and
    black monastic walls,
Of its red motors and lumbering trams, and self-
    sufficient people,
I will take you walking with me to a place you have not
    seen—
Half town and half country—the land of the Canal.
It is dearer to me than the antique town: I love it more
    than the rounded hills:
Straightest, sublimest of rivers is the long Canal.
I have observed great storms and trembled: I have wept
    for fear of the dark.
But nothing makes me so afraid as the clear water of this
    idle canal on a summer's noon.
Do you see the great telephone poles down in the water,
    how every wire is distinct?
If a body fell into the canal it would rest entangled in
    those wires for ever, between earth and air.
For the water is as deep as the stars are high.
One day I was thinking how if a man fell from that lofty
    pole

He would rush through the water toward me till his
    image was scattered by his splash,
When suddenly a train rushed by: the brazen dome of
    the engine flashed: the long white carriages roared;
The sun veiled himself for a moment, and the signals
    loomed in fog;
A savage woman screamed at me from a barge: little
    children began to cry;
The untidy landscape rose to life; a sawmill started;
A cart rattled down to the wharf, and workmen clanged
    over the iron footbridge;
A beautiful old man nodded from the first story window
    of a square red house,
And a pretty girl came out to hang up clothes in a small
    delightful garden.
O strange motion in the suburb of a county town: slow
    regular movement of the dance of death!
Men and not phantoms are these that move in light
Forgotten they live, and forgotten die.

HUMBERT WOLFE
1885–1940)

Born in Italy, Wolfe was educated at Bradford Grammar School and Wadham College, Oxford, before going on to a distinguished career as a Civil Servant, becoming (in 1938) deputy secretary to the Ministry of Labour. His accomplished work as both poet and critic was widely published in his lifetime.

Oxford

Some day I'll go back to Oxford—
I shall take the 4–50 from Paddington
(or its sweet ghost if it has ceased to run).
The porter will smile at my waistcoat and my ways,
when I'm not looking, as he used to in other days,
when I thought I was a man about town, and would
    stand
no nonsense, and he, I suppose, sniggered behind his
    hand.
I shall sit in my first class carriage (Everyone
travels first class to Oxford from Paddington,
except the Rhodes scholars, who never can
realize the responsibility of being an Oxford man).
At first I shall read without a trace of feeling,
and indicate a suitable contempt for Acton and Ealing.
I shall light a cigar, extremely black and thick
(and pray inwardly that it won't make me sick!)
And I shall languidly read over and again
the latest speech of Mr. Joseph Chamberlain.
I'll nod my head in careless assent to gall
the man in the corner, who looks like a Radical,
(If he isn't why does he get
stuff like 'The Star,' 'The Morning Leader' and 'The
    Westminster Gazette.'
I can understand giving the other side a chance,
but damn it! there are limits to tolerance!)

Then if I find that my acting is going badly,
and the old chap doesn't notice me, I'll take down
    Bradley,
and pretend to enjoy the 'Ethics,' and show the old fool
that, whatever he may be feeling, I am cool.
And that my blood doesn't jump like a fish, and shiver
with a soft deep sucking movement, into the river,
that I can just see, looking furtively sideways,
sweeping into the evening with haunted tideways,
and hidden under the woods that belt and crown it
with one white swan or two dream-floating down it.

I shall look perfectly calm, if anything calmer
than before, when we pass the works of Messrs. Huntley
    and Palmer.
And, while my heart will be wild like a groom at his
    wedding,
when the bride lifts her veil, I'll merely mutter 'Reading'
(And if the man in the corner looks up suddenly,
as though there was something that stirred his heart in
    me,
as though he guessed, and saw, and understood
how young I was, how glad, and found it good,
even though the fated end of boyhood, dim
with a brief beauty, clothed me, I'll strangle him.)

Didcot at last, Radley, and then still stiffly
(because perhaps he's watching) I'll look for Iffley.
Then I'll forget how old I am, and how wise,
and how remote from anything in the way of ecstasies,
because I shall see, like frozen lily-flowers
planted by a stone gardener of dreams, the Oxford
    towers.

I shall step out silently, and take a cab,
that slides along the cobbles like a wounded crab.
I'll say to the cabman 'Wadham,' and then sit
perfectly still, but my body will be lit

like a great house with candles. While I stare
steadily before me as though I didn't care.
Until we rattle up the Broad and clatter
into Parks Road. And nothing then will matter.
The college windows will be lit, and someone will shout:
'Good Lord! here's Wolfe again,' and I'll get out,
and pass through the college gateway into the Quad.
Some day I'll go back to Oxford.

SIR JOHN BETJEMAN
(1906–1984)

The son of a furniture designer and manufacturer, Betjeman was educated at Marlborough and Magdalen College, Oxford—where he failed to take a degree. After a brief career as a schoolmaster he became assistant editor of the *Architectural Review*. He also worked in the publicity department of Shell, being responsible for the *Shell Guides* to the counties of England. He was later a very popular and accomplished broadcaster, notably in a series of documentaries on architectural subjects. A noted conservationist, he founded the Victorian Society in 1958. He was awarded a CBE in 1960, and a knighthood in 1969. He was also awarded an honorary D.Litt by the University of Oxford, and held honorary Fellowships at both Keble and Magdalen Colleges. He was made Poet Laureate in 1972. He wrote a number of other poems on Oxford themes, notably 'Oxford: Sudden Illness at the Bus-stop','Myfanwy at Oxford', 'On an Old-Fashioned Water-Colour of Oxford', 'May-Day Song for North Oxford', and 'I.M. Walter Ramsden ob. March 26, 1947 Pembroke College, Oxford'. There are amusing and relevant passages in *Summoned by Bells* (1960), too. His poem on the church of St Barnabas is remembered by Jonathan Price later in this anthology.

St. Barnabas, Oxford

How long was the peril, how breathless the day,
In topaz and beryl, the sun dies away,
His rays lying static at quarter to six
On polychromatical lacing of bricks.
Good Lord, as the angelus floats down the road
Byzantine St. Barnabas, be Thine Abode.

Where once the fritillaries hung in the grass
A baldachin's pillar is guarding the Mass.
Farewell to blue meadows we loved not enough,
And elms in whose shadows were Glanville and Clough
Not poets but clergymen hastened to meet
Thy redden'd remorselessness, Cardigan Street.

Church of England thoughts occasioned by hearing the
bells of Magdalen Tower, from the Botanic Garden,
Oxford on St. Mary Magdalen's Day

I see the urn against the yew,
    The sunlit urn of sculptured stone,
I see its shapely shadow fall
On this enormous garden wall
    Which makes a kingdom of its own.

A grassy kingdom sweet to view
    With tiger lilies still in flower
And beds of umbelliferæ
Ranged in Linnaean symmetry,
    All in the sound of Magdalen tower.

A multiplicity of bells,
    A changing cadence, rich and deep
Swung from those pinnacles on high
To fill the trees and flood the sky
    And rock the sailing clouds to sleep.

A Church of England sound, it tells
    Of "moderate" worship, God and State,
Where matins congregations go
Conservative and good and slow
    To elevations of the plate.

And loud through resin-scented chines
    And purple rhododendrons roll'd,
I hear the bells for Eucharist
From churches blue with incense mist
    Where reredoses twinkle gold.

Chapels-of-ease by railway lines
    And humble streets and smells of gas
I hear your plaintive ting-tangs call
From many a gabled western wall
    To Morning Prayer or Holy Mass.

In country churches old and pale
    I hear the changes smoothly rung
And watch the coloured sallies fly
From rugged hands to rafters high
    As round and back the bells are swung.

Before the spell begins to fail,
    Before the bells have lost their power,
Before the grassy kingdom fade
And Oxford traffic roar invade,
    I thank the bells of Magdalen Tower.

MAIDA STANIER

(1909–1991)

Maida Stanier was the daughter of an Edinburgh schoolmaster. After gaining a first in Classics at Edinburgh University, she married Bob Stanier, who was for many years a distinguished Master of Magdalen College School in Oxford. She wrote several radio plays and made frequent broadcasts about the history of Oxford for Radio Oxford. She also published a novel, *The Singing Time*. She was best known, however, as a writer of light verse. For almost twenty years, under the pen name of Culex, she contributed fortnightly poems to the *Oxford Times*, poking gentle fun at Oxford dignitaries.

Two Portraits
Don—Old Style

Here hangs an eighteenth century don
For all the world to look upon.
A bachelor, who all the same
Kept a convenient 'wife' at Thame.
Learned a little, shrewd no less,
He published at the Sheldon Press
(In Turkish leather) one small book;
Which done, his Fellowship he took
As a reward for toil; he said
No *gentleman* should write for bread
But none need apprehend starvation
Who can turn off a dedication.
To gossip round the coffee-houses
With sly, occasional carouses
Was his delight in any season.
He loved his fellow men (in reason)
But tempered loving with despising.
His tastes were all for sermonising
So that he met his Great Eclipse
With dogma at his fingertips,
Greeting death calmly as a friend.
He made a very pious end.

Don—New Style

Here hangs a twentieth century don,
A rather harassed Casaubon.
A married man to chores resigned,
His home is the 'progressive' kind.
A scholar in the narrow way
That specialists pursue today,
He'll write most willingly for pay;
Nor scorns to gild the spoken word
With small assignments on the Third,
Which with his pupils ranks as fame.
(They call him by his Christian name
As is the idiom of their age.)
Sometimes he vents a donnish rage
On other dons. The S.C.R.
Has known that mettle which in war
Won him a ribbon. But when able
He likes to dine at the High Table,
The humble servant of his college,
Who knows he knows not, which is knowledge.
His standing's good with friends and foes.
But how he stands with God—who knows?

ANNE RIDLER
(b.1912)

Anne Ridler was educated at Downe House School and King's College, London. From 1935 to 1940 she was a member of the editorial department at Faber and Faber. Her first collection (*Poems*) was published by Oxford University Press in 1939; her *Collected Poems* appeared from Carcanet in 1994. Responding to the models of T. S. Eliot and Charles Williams, she has made important contributions to the tradition of verse drama in the twentieth century. She has also made several distinguished translations of Italian libretti and has edited works by Williams and a major edition of the writings of Thomas Traherne (OUP, 1966).

Pegasus in the Botanical Gardens

So we came . . .
To a place where three ways and two seasons met,
In spring at the edge of Oxford.
'Here,' said the Fox, 'is a city of screaming tyres,
Where lorries piled with motor-shells
Fly like clumsy Maybugs through the streets,
And the river drumbles past exotic barges.
The smoke of learning rises with the river-mists
And spires like funnels carry praise to heaven.
Thin and rare is the rising praise
But the heavenly thought descends in flesh and blood.
Once with tremendous wings vanning the sky
It seemed a flying horse, and prayed for, came
To kill the chimaera of men's dismal fears;
Then sprang, like a diver rising from the depths, to
      Olympus,
Throwing its rider, who would have ridden to heaven
But had not learnt its horsemanship . . .'

I crossed the bridge, with the whirling wrack of traffic.
The sky was laid below me in azure anemones,
The willows wept against the sun like rainbows
And punts as lazy as clouds slipped by beneath.

I came to the double gateway
Where the Stuarts guard the tranquil garden,
The chimes fall among rare plants like rain
And blackened ashlar walls debar
The rabble of 'prams and all disorderly persons'.
A wolf and boar of stone
Sat snarling back on their haunches,
And the Horse of the wind-outpacing thought
Quietly fed there, tasting
The luculent waxen blooms
Of the leafless magnolia tree...

JOHN HEATH-STUBBS

(b.1918)

John Heath-Stubbs was educated at Bembridge School, Worcester College for the Blind, and Queen's College, Oxford, being awarded his BA in 1942; his first collection (*Wounded Thammuz*) was published in the same year. He has been prolific—and highly accomplished— as poet, editor, and critic ever since. Carcanet published his *Collected Poems 1943–1987* in 1988, and further collections have appeared since. His many awards include the Queen's Gold Medal for Poetry (1973) and the Commonwealth Poetry Prize (1989). He was awarded an OBE in 1989. 'Addison's Walk' is the third poem in his sequence 'The Heart's Forest'.

Addison's Walk

Grove, and you, trees, by careless birds
   Frequented, and you fronds, impersonal,
   Whose greenness soothed the long intestine broil
   Within my head, when I would seek your shades

Those former months of solitude, remembering
   That sane cool mind who christened you, quietly,
   In his discreet and formal century
   Beside the unhurried river's marge walking;
   Now that together in the season's prime

We've come this way, marked the symbolic flowers,
   And the axe striking on the murdered willows,
   When this is over, and the wing of time
   Has brushed aside desire, in after years
   Returning here, what ghosts will haunt these
     shadows?

ELIZABETH JENNINGS

(b.1926)

Born in Lincolnshire, Elizabeth Jennings was educated at Oxford High School for Girls and St Anne's College, Oxford. She has lived in Oxford for many years. Like a number of other Oxford poets of the period, she had her first small collection published by the Fantasy Press, in 1953. A substantial selection of her work from 1953 to 1985 was published as *Collected Poems* (Carcanet, 1986), a volume which won the 1987 W. H. Smith Literary Award. 'Spell of Oxford' is the first of a sequence of sixteen poems, published as *An Oxford Cycle* in 1987.

Spell of Oxford

It is a scheme of spires
A haze of green
A range of clouds
A cluster of boys
And girls and the old
Who move in a trance
Of learning and love
Knowledge and power
There is also peace
In the dark green streams
Where the punts glide
And the willows fall
In Summer and Spring
The young are a-dance
In-between lectures
The rush of learning
Hubbub of parties
It is time out of time
In three terms
It will last you all life
In a glamour of dreams

ANTHONY THWAITE
(b.1930)

Born in Chester, Thwaite read English at Christ Church after two years of military service in Libya. He has worked as an academic in Japan, Libya, and Kuwait; as a radio producer with the BBC; as literary editor of *The Listener* and the *New Statesman*; and as one of the editors of *Encounter* from 1973 to 1985. He has also worked for the publishers Secker and Warburg and André Deutsch. His earliest collection was published in Oxford by the Fantasy Press in 1953. Important later collections include *The Stones of Emptiness* (1967) and *Victorian Voices* (1980)—from which impressive sequence 'After High Table' is taken. Much of Thwaite's best work is characterized by his striking historical imagination.

After High Table
(Oxford, c.1870)

Hockley is turning Papist, so they say
His set is stiff with incense, and he bobs
Most roguishly in chapel. More and more
The Whore of Babylon extends her sway.
Branston is fiddling with his 'little jobs',
Copying the Bursar's buttery accounts
Into a pocket book he locks away.
In Common Room each night, the floor
Is held by Foxton, face flushed like a plum
About to drop—and we have seen him drop
Drunk as a carter in the smouldering grate.
They are all here, my *Corpus Asinorum*,
Donkeys in orders, stuffed in jowl and crop.
One day it will be said 'He did the state
Some service', when they read my book of fools.

The Master's slack. He does not know the rules.
He is—can't be denied—a natural curate
And would be better suited to the cure
Of souls in Wiltshire, ministering to pigs.
I've seen old Figgins watch him like a ferret,
For Figgins was passed over, and for sure
Preferment went because Enthusiasts

175

Clamoured for someone without Roman views.
But—pardon me—the Master strokes and frigs
His conscience like a trollop with an itch
Flat on her back and panting in the stews.
All pious mush dressed up as manliness,
Evangelistic canting, keen to bring
Trousers to niggers who don't wear a stitch.
A man's religion is his own. To sing
Barnstorming stanzas to the Lord's as poor
As Newman fluting eunuch fancyings,
His heavenly choir on earth. O that old Whore,
How devious she becomes!

                              This elm-smoke stings
My eyes at night, when I should be holed up
Snugly behind the bulwark of my oak.
Some more Marsala, or another cup
Of punch . . . What frowsty collared priest is this,
Another chum of Kingston's on the soak
Or snivelling gaitered surrogate from Bath?
Give me your arm—I needs must go and piss.

My colleagues all tread down the primrose path
That—who?—oh, Shakespeare then—put in a play.
I should be even now, I tell you, hard
Pent in my room and working at my book,
Theocritus, my text, my elegiac
Pagan . . .

   How these chatterers swill and stay!
I'll take a turn with you around the yard,
The farther quad where dotards never look,
Or if they do, then always back and back
To the dark backward and abysm of time . . .
But then we are all backward-lookers here,

If you would understand me: relicts, men
Who hear the echo when we hear the chime,
As Great Tom stuns the silence. In my ear
I sense the falter of the tolling bell,
I hear it boom again, again, again,
Fetching me back and back, not boding well,
And the full moon hangs high across St Ebbe's . . .

Where was I? Morbid, maybe, at this hour
When Master, Bursar, Chaplain, Dean and all
Waddle like corpulent spiders in their webs
To winding staircases and narrow beds,
To livings without life, posts without power,
A benefice without a benefit.
I have you all marked down . . .

JONATHAN PRICE

(1931–1985)

Jonathan Price was educated at Kingswood School, Bath and, after National Service in the RAF, read English at Lincoln College, Oxford. He made a career in publishing, joining Oxford University Press in 1964. Along with Anthony Thwaite, he edited *Oxford Poetry*, published by the Fantasy Press in 1954. In the same year the Fantasy Press published a selection of Price's own work. His most substantial collection of poems, *Everything Must Go*, was published by Secker and Warburg in 1985.

Sir John Revisits Jericho

I wander first down Cranham Street
To where Canal Street still may go,
And mark, in every face I meet,
Marks of change in Jericho.

Among white faces black, brown, yellow
Stare at me as if to say
Here's a curious-looking fellow,
Probably he's lost his way.

True, the place and I are older;
But, a poet-pilgrim, I
Come to many such sites bolder
And not proud to wonder why.

Much has changed since my last visit
Fifteen, twenty years ago.
Here comes Hart Street now, so is it
Albert next? I used to know.

Two up, two down, with small back gardens,
Houses stood here in decent rows;
And perhaps the Lord, who pardons
Worse crimes, pardons Jericho's.

Redevelopment, they term it:
Eloquent mute annals must
At the flourish of a permit
Tumble and vanish, dust to dust.

To Canal Street now I come
Burning with eagerness to see
Saint Barnabas: and am struck dumb,
Almost, when it towers over me.

Functional High Church Byzantine,
You are but rubble trimmed with brick
(Blomfield, eighteen sixty-nine);
So bless, good Barnabas, the pick

Knocking humbler walls asunder
To the strains of Radio Two.
May its wielder pause and wonder
Whose the hand that plumbed the loo;

May he take a last look round
At the flowered bedroom wall
And, before it hits the ground,
Reck his own decline and fall.

Bulldozers roar here today,
And tomorrow will be gone.
Time will bear us all away
With Blomfield and the mastodon.

Yet forgive the City planners
For they half know what they do:
Architectural good manners
Stop them making all things new.

In Council housing snug beside
Victorian pub and corner shop
Oxford can take a modest pride:
Someone at least knows when to stop.

Will others mark, and mend their ways?
Where spectral shepherds watch ghost flocks
Arrogant ARIBAs
Blight the earth with concrete blocks.

Developers behind them stand:
On tax-loss farms with whited gates
In greener and more pleasant land
They contemplate the mortgage rates . . .

But I am due to dine in Town
And must cut short my peroration.
Farewell, dear Oxford! Hat-brim down,
I set off briskly for the station.

ANNE STEVENSON
(b.1933)

Anne Stevenson was born in England (in Cambridge), but grew up in America, where she was educated at the University of Michigan and the Radcliffe Institute in Cambridge, Massachusetts. A varied career as teacher, academic, writer, and bookseller has taken her to many parts of the USA and Britain (where she has lived for more than twenty-five years). She was a Fellow of Lady Margaret Hall, 1975–77. Her earliest collection (*Living in America*) was published in Ann Arbor in 1965. Important later collections include *Correspondences* (1974), *Travelling Behind Glass: Selected Poems 1963–1973* (1974), *Enough of Green* (1977), *Minute by Glass Minute* (1982), *The Fiction-Makers* (1985), and *The Other House* (1990). They show a constantly developing poet, never content to repeat herself. *Bitter Fame*, Stevenson's biography of Sylvia Plath, was published in 1989. Other Oxford poems by Stevenson include 'By the Boat House, Oxford' and 'Temporarily in Oxford'—both in her *Collected Poems, 1955–1995* (OUP, 1996).

Dreaming of (More) Spires

When I am rich

I'm going to endow a college in Oxford
called Lost Souls College.

The Fellows will be specialists in Despair.

Also, I suspect, a number of Fellowesses
will find themselves there.

For the permanently drunk
there'll be the usual privileges and places.
But for dirty old men whose bunks
are streets, whose chairs are drafty hedges,
there'll be beds, baths, heating, glasses
and maybe even built-in shelves for haloes and crosses.

Practical suicide will be offered, as well as classes
in Snobology and Anathematics.

Chairs in Metafailure and Gastrophysics
will be two attractions,
but the highest and grandest chair (don't you agree)
should be the Regius Professorship of Simple and
    Compound Factions.

The architecture? Well, we'll see.
We might have caves of ice in the manner of Coleridge.
We might buy up that redbrick Venetian confection
next to Folly Bridge.
Whatever we decide, in the largest, most touristical
    cloister
a sculpture made of lost bikes, failed theses, fag-ends
red tape and refused applications for grants
will stand as a monument to our patron philosopher,
I Kant.

There will also be a garden
dedicated to the use of such poetical men and women
as are too easily lost or discouraged in the Forest of
    Auden.

Lovers of all sexes
will be accommodated *gratis*.
But when, with its petty pace, the Worm of Time creeps
    in
(with all that blether about tomorrow and tomorrow and
    tomorrow)
we'll remember the Lost Souls chaplain and invite him
    in
to preach on Resignation and the Wages of Gin.

The Professor of Poetry, kind and vain,
might be a Fellow.

The warden could be called John Sorrow.

JOHN FULLER

(b.1937)

Son of the distinguished poet (and Oxford Professor of Poetry) Roy Fuller, John Fuller was educated at St Paul's School and New College, Oxford. He won the Newdigate Prize in 1960. Since 1966 he has been a Fellow of Magdalen College, Oxford. His earliest collection of poems, *Fairground Music*, was published by Chatto and Windus in 1961. His *Collected Poems* appeared (from the same publishers) in 1996. He has also had considerable success as a novelist, and his important *W.H. Auden: a commentary* was published in 1998. The Upper Reading Room in the Bodleian Library is home to those undertaking research in English or History.

Upper reading room: six p.m.

In the guilty half-silence of this long
Waiting-room, allusions buzz for us
Like flies, chairs scrape back for topics leaving
From a different platform. Lugging each hero's baggage,
We lie: 'I am like you. You are alive in me.'

Kipper-tied quinquagenarians, tramps
With satchels, academic teeny-boppers
Their carrels piled with hats and avacados,
Knee-locked civil servants of apparatus,
Nuns: we are shades that have lasted one more day.

And our eyes meet over the low partitions
In tentative love, sharing our furtive sense
Of the insults of that antagonist with whom
We ever contrive grandmaster draws, who sets
The problems that we compromise, from whom

We all on some long morning learned the rules.
He stains the stones. The scaffold streams with him.
Leggy girls on their venerable monosyllables
Are led by him to a gagging dryness. Boys
Smooth their balding heads, invoking his praises.

He brings the wrinkled clean expatriates
To the dug-outs of a mad ambition, shading
Their narrowed eyes on the beaches of exegesis,
Saying" 'We will return.' He likes to see
A gulping of tesseracts and Gondals in

Our crazed search across sands of the impossible
For the undying, and he annotates
Pistacia terebinthus to a sacrament,
Its sweet stench long evaporated
In the pages of a demythologised

Indexed kerygma. But we refuse to be bullied,
Even as hammers slog the walls crumbling
Around us. Books are about life, and life
Is somewhere here. On paper. In eyes. Somewhere.
So now we stack our cards. We reserve our defence.

FRANCIS WARNER

(b.1937)

Born in Yorkshire, Francis Warner was educated at Christ's Hospital, the London College of Music, and St Catharine's College, Cambridge. Since 1965 he has been Fellow in English Literature at St Peter's College, Oxford. His *Collected Poems 1960–1984* was published in 1985, and his *Agora: an Epic*, a series of historical dramas, appeared in 1994.

I Saw A Shining Lady

I saw a shining lady stand,
In fields I could not recognize.
Caught unawares in a strange land
I stared at where a path would rise
    Across a nettled wilderness
    Shadowing ruin's emptiness.

I saw her walk on crumbling rocks
(How near to heaven I could not gauge)
But softening her barefoot shocks
Five-petalled meadow-saxifrage
    Wove yellow buttons and long stems,
    Like buttercups beside the Thames.

The red herb-Robert twined a bridge
With celandine and town-hall-clocks
Across the hard, uneven ridge
That marked decay of walls and locks,
    Roof, windows, bricks turned back to loam
    That constituted once a home.

And all my heart was filled with light
To see how she was safely held,
The stones themselves stirred with delight
And tears behind my eyelids welled.
    But when they cleared once more I found
    The Oxford traffic all around.

SALLY PURCELL
(1944–1998)

Sally Purcell was an undergraduate at Lady Margaret Hall, obtaining her BA in 1966 and her MA in 1970. In a contribution to a reference work, Purcell said simply, 'I was brought up a classicist, and I believe in courtesy, craftsmanship and honesty.' Such qualities mark the best of her work as a poet and translator, work which was gaining wider recognition at the time of her premature death.

Oxford, Early Michaelmas Term

Impossible to register
each delicacy & shade,
each further richness of affectation
this feminine season adopts
for an audience captivated in advance
& hypnotised by hearsay, by skilful propaganda,
by its longing to play Hamlet
and be *really* melancholy.

Confident flirtations with a preciosity
already near to over-ripeness
increase the delight in imagined possession
of the inherited magic world;
whose soul and typewriter will vibrate first
to appraise in College garden
some sere and yellow leaf,
as the aesthetes flower gently?

CRAIG RAINE
(b.1944)

Born in Bishop Auckland, County Durham, Craig Raine was educated at Barnard Castle School and Exeter College, Oxford. From 1981 to 1991 he was poetry editor at Faber and Faber. He is currently Fellow in English at New College, Oxford. His main collections of poetry are *The Onion, Memory* (1978), *A Martian Sends a Postcard Home* (1979), *Rich* (1984), *History: The Home Movie* (1994), and *Clay. Whereabouts Unknown* (1996). A collection of literary essays, *Haydn and the Valve Trumpet*, was published in 1990. Raine's other poems on Oxford subjects include 'The Fair in St. Giles' and 'Jew the Obscure' (both in *The Onion, Memory*) and several sections in *History: The Home Movie*.

Houses in North Oxford

are on parade, inspected by the sun
who looks them in the eyes and strikes
his medals on the spot . . .

Row on row of red-brick guards,
with window boxes boasting battle ribbons
from the Spring campaign. They stand

at attention: the cars a line of
impeccable boots, all at an angle
of one hundred and eighty degrees;

bay windows bulging like holsters;
rifles clamped to their sides.
Not one soldier moves, unless

you happen to see the slow
confident wink of a blind being drawn . . .
The gardens lay out kit—

spick privet, polished laurels,
the larch's tiny hand grenades,
pipe-clayed lilies of the valley—

while Keble sprawls at ease, handsome
in mufti, the general in Fair-Isles,
his Sam Browne dangling like a fire-escape.

Who would guess from this the timed heart—
the wounded professor, nuns on their knees,
the dear old thing afraid of a khaki envelope?

DUNCAN BUSH
(b.1946)

Born in Cardiff, Duncan Bush studied at Warwick University, at Duke University in North Carolina, and at Oxford. His collections of poetry include *Aquarium* (1983), *Salt* (1985), and *Masks* (1994). *The Hook* (1997) is a substantially revised reprint of *Aquarium* and *Salt*. 'The Colleges' is the first of a three-poem sequence of 'Oxford Poems', the others being 'Outside the Hospital' and 'The New Estate'.

The Colleges

After all these years, this place believes
In its myth. Outside, bright air burns colder.
The late afternoon intensifies. Golder
The sun gilds yellow stone and mottled leaves

Of tinted, tainted elms dying in drifts
On college lawns. Indian Summer will soon pass
Into another term, another Michaelmas.
High, in Agfacolour blue, the last swifts

Wheel, while visitors stroll quadrangles, to stare
In at small austerities of privilege—
The draughty common sink, the crumbling edge
Of Cotswold sills, the old decrepit stair—

Glimpsed in the tourism of mere spending-power,
Vicariousness on pilgrimage. While Nikons click
At Magdalen's deer, or Keble's Fairisle-pattern brick,
Even our own eyes mist at the worn step, arch, tower

Long blurred by envy, arrivisme, regret
In our own complex retrograde emotions
For a lifestyle of which life here lends us notions,
Nostalgia for false worlds we've never met,
Yet to which so many hunger to belong—
All still persisting through a silvered, Georgian haze
Across meadows, trees heavy with shade: such days
As only Oxford's midsummers prolong.

189

Index of sources used

LODGE: *Scillaes Metamorphosis* (1589); HARINGTON: *The most elegant and witty epigrams (1618)*; DRAYTON: 'The Fifteenth Song', *Polyolbion* (1612); DANIEL: *The Complete Works* (1855); DAVIES: *The Scourge of Folly* (1611); GAMAGE: *Linsie-woolsie* (1613); CORBETT: B.L. Add MS 30982; BRATHWAITE: *Barnabœ Itinerarium (1638)*, *Times curtaine drawne* (1621); HOWELL: *Poems*, by William Cartwright (1651); STRODE: Walter Porter, *Madrigals and Ayres* (1632): BENLOWES: *Oxonii Encomium* (1672); MILTON / COWPER: Cowper, *Works* (1835–37); CARTWRIGHT: *Poems* (1651); COWLEY: *English Writings* (1905–06); LLUELYN: *Men-Miracles* (1646); HEATH: *Clarastella, together with Poems occasional, Elegies, Epigrams, Satyrs* (1650); VAUGHAN: *Thalia Rediviva* (1678); BOLD: *Poems* (1664); DRYDEN: *Miscellany Poems: By the most Eminent Hands* (1684); ALDRICH: *English Songs: Dryden and His Times*, ed. E. Arber (n.d.); LEIGH: *Poems, Upon Several Occasions* (1675); FLATMAN: *Poems and Songs* (1686); BROWN: *Works* (1760); GLANVIL: *Poems* (1725); D'ANVERS: *Academia: or, the Humours of the University of Oxford, in burlesque Verse* (1691); EVANS: *Vertumnus: An Epistle to Mr. Jacob Bobart* (1713); TRAPP / BROWNE: John Nichols, *Literary Anecdotes of the Eighteenth Century (1812–15)* ; WOODWARD: *Poems on Several Occasions* (1730); TICKELL: *Poems* (1810); AMHURST: *Poems on Several Occasions (1723)*, *Strephon's Revenge* (1720); MASON: *The Poems* (1822); WARTON: *The Poetical Works* (1802); ANONYMOUS: *Gentleman's Magazine* (November 1767); BISHOP: *The Poetical Works* (1796); BATHURST: British Library, Add. MS 61910; MAURICE: *Poems* (1779); POLWHELE: *The Follies of Oxford* (1785); BOWLES: *The Poetical Works* (1855); HEADLEY: *Poems* (1786); WORDSWORTH: *The Poetical Works* (1849–50); SOUTHEY: *The Poetical Works* (1845); ANONYMOUS: *Notes and Queries*, Second Series, XI, March 2nd 1861, p. 170; KEATS: *The Poetical Works and Other Writings* (1883); HAWKER: *The Poetical Works* (1899); BEDDOES: *The Poems* (1851); MONTGOMERY: *Oxford: Or, Alma Mater* (1831); FABER: *Poems* (1857); CASWALL: *Hymns and Poems* (1873); M. ARNOLD: *Macmillan's Magazine* (April, 1866); THORNBURY: *Historical & Legendary Ballads & Songs* (1876); E. ARNOLD: *The Secret of Death* (1885); WATTS-DUNTON: *The Coming of Love* (1906); WARD: *Confessions of a Poet* (1894); HOPKINS: *Poems* (1918); BOURDILLON: *Among the*

Flowers (1878), *Miniscula* (1897); WILDE: *The Works* (1909); BEECHING: *Balliol Rhymes* (1881), *Mensae Secvndae* (1879); SPRING-RICE: *Balliol Rhymes* (1881); NESBIT: *Songs of Love and Empire* (1898); JOHNSON: *Poetical Works* (1915); ANONYMOUS: *Oxford Magazine* (1894); FLECKER: *Collected Poems* (1916); WOLFE: *The Unknown Goddess* (1925); BETJEMAN: *Collected Poems* (1970); STANIER: *Ten Oxford Poets: An Anthology* (1978); RIDLER: Collected Poems (1994); HEATH-STUBBS: *Collected Poems, 1943–1987* (1988); JENNINGS: *An Oxford Cycle* (1987); THWAITE: *Victorian Voices* (1980); PRICE: *Everything Must Go* (1985); STEVENSON: *Ten Oxford Poets: An Anthology* (1978); FULLER: *Collected Poems* (1996); WARNER: *Collected Poems 1960–1984* (1985); PURCELL: *The Holly Queen* (1971); RAINE: *The Onion, Memory* (1978); BUSH: *The Hook* (1997).

Acknowledgements

The editors would like to thank Roger Lonsdale, for his suggestion of 'The Oxonian' by Thomas Maurice; Tom Stanier, for providing biographical information about his mother, Maida Stanier; Sandra Raphael, for her expert copy-editing and proof-reading of the typescript; Henrietta Leyser; Anne Ridler; and Hugo Brunner, for his general advice, help, and support.

Copyright acknowledgements:

'Church of England Thoughts...'; 'St. Barnabas Oxford'. John Betjeman: *Collected Poems*, John Murray, 1962.

'The Colleges'. Duncan Bush: *The Hook*. Seren, 1997.

'Upper reading room: six. p.m.' John Fuller: *Collected Poems*, Chatto & Windus, 1996.

'Addison's Walk'. John Heath-Stubbs: *Collected Poems: 1943–1987*, Carcanet Press, 1988.

'Spell of Oxford'. Elizabeth Jennings: *An Oxford Cycle*. Thorntons, 1987.

'Sir John Revisits Jericho'. Jonathan Price: *Everything Must Go*. Secker and Warburg, 1985.

'Oxford, Early Michaelmas Term', is taken from *The Holly Queen* by Sally Purcell, Anvil Press, 1971.

'Houses in North Oxford'. © Craig Raine 1978. Reprinted from *The Onion, Memory* by Craig Raine (1978) by permission of Oxford University Press.

'Pegasus in the Botanical Gardens', from 'The Golden Bird'. Anne Ridler: *Collected Poems*. Carcanet Press, 1994.

© Tom Stanier. 'Don—Old Style'; 'Don—New Style'. Maida Stanier: *Ten Oxford Poets*. Charles Brand, 1978.

'Dreaming of (More) Spires'. Anne Stevenson: *Ten Oxford Poets*. Charles Brand, 1978.

© Anthony Thwaite. 'After High Table'. Anthony Thwaite: *Selected Poems 1956–1996*. Enitharmon Press, 1997.

'I Saw a Shining Lady'. Francis Warner: *Collected Poems 1960–1984*. Colin Smythe, 1985.

'Oxford', reprinted by permission of The Peters Fraser and Dunlop Group Limited; as printed in the original volume, *The Unknown Goddess*, by Humbert Wolfe.